MUCH ADO ABOUT NOTHING

In series with this book

Also edited by Dr J. H. Walter

HENRY V (Arden Shakespeare)

CHARLEMAGNE (Malone Society)

LAUNCHING OF THE MARY (Malone Society)

MUCH ADO ABOUT NOTHING

Edited by
J. H. WALTER
M.A., PH.D.

Fellow of University College London
Formerly Headmaster
Minchenden School, Southgate

Heinemann is an imprint of Pearson
Education Limited, a company incorporated in England
and Wales, having its registered office at Edinburgh Gate, Harlow,
Essex, CM20 2JE. Registered company number: 872828

Heinemann is a registered trademark of Pearson Education Limited

ISBN: 978 0 435190 12 5

17

First American edition published by
Plays, Inc. 1979

Library of Congress Cataloging in Publication Data

Shakespeare, William, 1564–1616.
  Much ado about nothing.

  (The players' Shakespeare)
  SUMMARY: Presents the comedy of two couples who are happily
united with the help of bumbling Constable Dogberry. Includes com-
mentary on each page of the text.
  [1. Shakespeare, William, 1564–1616. Much ado about nothing.   2.
Plays]   I. Walter, John Henry.   II. Title.
PR2828.A2W34   1979   822.3'3   79-14925
ISBN 0–8238–0238–8

Printed in China (CTPS/17)

CONTENTS

PREFACE

THE aim of this edition is to encourage pupils to study the play as a play, not as a novel or a narrative, but as a pattern of speech and movement creating an artistic whole. While it has been generally accepted that this approach stimulates and enlivens classroom work, it has more recently become clear that it is a most fruitful way of preparing for examinations. Reports issued by the University of Cambridge Local Examinations Syndicate call attention to this aspect in the work of examination candidates. The following comments are taken from an Advanced Level report:

'It will be seen that the best candidates are often those who show themselves conscious of the play as a made thing -- usually, but by no means always, as a thing made for the theatre.' Again, 'And perhaps the most misunderstood aspect of Shakespeare is the part played by theatrical convention'.

The interleaved notes, therefore, in addition to a gloss, interpretations of character, dialogue, and imagery, considered particularly from the point of view of a play. There are some suggestions for acting, for the most part simple pointers to avoid rigidity of interpretation and drawn up with an apron stage in mind. Some questions are interposed to provide topics for discussion or to assist in discrimination.

It is suggested that the play should be read through rapidly with as little comment as possible. In a second reading the notes should be used in detail, and appropriate sections of the Introduction might be read at the teacher's discretion.

It is hoped that this edition will enable the teacher to take his class more deeply into the play than the usual meagre allowance of time permits him to do; it is not an attempt to usurp his function.

I

Preface

I gratefully acknowledge help in preparing this edition from a considerable number of studies of *Much Ado About Nothing*. From them I give a list of books which may help the student:

R. Berry, *Shakespeare's Comedies*
J. R. Brown, *Shakespeare and his Comedies*
L. S. Champion, *The Evolution of Shakespeare's Comedy*
B. Evans, *Shakespeare's Comedies*
R. G. Hunter, *Shakespeare and the Comedy of Forgiveness*
P. A. Jorgensen, *Redeeming Shakespeare's Words*
M. M. Mahood, *Shakespeare's Wordplay*
J. R. Mulryne, *Shakespeare: Much Ado About Nothing*
A. P. Rossiter, *Angel with Horns*

C. T. Prouty, *The Sources of 'Much Ado About Nothing'* is very useful but not easily obtainable.

There is a stimulating article by D. Ormerod in *Shakespeare Survey 25*. To this and to articles by J. A. Barish, A. Leggatt, G. Storey I am much indebted.

I am grateful to my wife who has given me considerable help in gathering material, clarifying thought, and correcting errors; to Jeanne Gooding for her time and care in typing copy; and to Edward Burrough for his investigation of French farces and his suggestion incorporated in Appendix II.

Biblical quotations are from the *Bishops' Bible* (1575), unless otherwise stated, with the spelling modernized. References to Shakespeare's plays not published in this series follow the line numbering of the Globe edition.

INTRODUCTION

I

TEXT

THE first edition of the play, the quarto edition (Q), was published in 1600 apparently with the consent of Shakespeare's company. The manuscript copy for Q was Shakespeare's 'foul papers', that is the author's final draft from which a fair copy would be made to serve as the prompt-copy in the theatre. Q text has a number of inconsistencies and shortcomings of a kind likely to occur in an author's draft because of alterations, corrections, abbreviations, and changes of mind, particularly over characters, and hence in entry directions. Some of these contain the names of characters who have no part in the play: Innogen, Leonato's wife (I.i; II.i), or in the scene: Balthasar (I.i.82), John, Borachio and Conrade (II.i.190). Names vary: Don Pedro is sometimes Don Peter (I.i.1,9), or Prince (II.i.74, 190); Dogberry and Verges are sometimes Constable and Headborough (III.v.1), and sometimes referred to by the names, Kempe and Cowley, of the actors who played the parts (IV.ii). There are other lesser irregularities.

The compositor who set Q misread some speech headings (II.i.74; IV.i.4). It is known from his work elsewhere that, failing to remember the exact words of his copy, he substituted words that made sense. Probably 'dead' for 'dumb' (V.iii.10) is such a substitution, but there may be many others that it is not possible to detect.

The Folio edition (F) of Shakespeare's plays (1623) was

3

printed from a copy of Q which had been slightly amended by reference to the manuscript theatre prompt book.

This edition is based on Q as being closest to Shakespeare's words, but a few readings from F have been preferred.

II

PERFORMANCE

Much Ado About Nothing was probably first performed towards the end of 1598 or early 1599 for it is not mentioned in the list of Shakespeare's plays in Meres' *Palladis Tamia*, published during autumn 1598. The names of two actors, Kempe and Cowley, for Dogberry and Verges in speech-headings in IV.ii indicate that the play was composed before Kempe left the company late in 1599. The first record of a performance is an entry in the *Chamber Account* of payments on 20 May 1613 to the King's Players for performances of 'Benedicte and Betteris' at Whitehall during the festivities at the wedding of Princess Elizabeth to the Elector Palatine.

The play was popular. There was reference to it in other plays from 1600 onwards. Ben Jonson in his *Bartholomew Fair* (1614) notes imitations: 'and then a substantial watch to have stolen in upon them, and taken them away with mistaking words, as the fashion is in stage practice'. Indeed, before the closing of the theatres in 1642 at least nine plays imitated it by introducing a constable and watch, usually a constable who lacked wit and slept on duty. By that time the phrase 'wit in a constable' was established to denote an absurdity.

III

GENERAL

Much Ado About Nothing, like other Shakespearian comedies, deals with the love and friendships of two pairs of young lovers attached to the court of a prince or duke in a Mediter-ranean city. Intermingled are clown-like, native English watchmen whose blunderings unconsciously parody and criticize some of the main characters. There is a self-confessed villain. Instrumental and vocal music celebrate festivity, fore-shadow a theme, emphasize a mood and a reconciliation. In short the play follows the old principle that a comedy begins in trouble, ends in joy, and is centred in love.

Praise for the play's structure has been unstinting. Its epi-sodes and characters are most elegantly and deftly integrated into a symmetrical whole. It contains eight 'devices' or 'prac-tices' that influence or change attitudes, and which lead to specific actions involving the playing of parts, and to eaves-droppings. Six of these devices employ some form of decep-tion, five involve overhearing. In addition to the two anti-thetical plots of the lovers there are balanced episodes: the masquing, dancing, and choosing of a bride in II.i with the masquing, choosing of brides, and dancing in V.iv; the arbour scene in II.iii with that in III.i. The rejection scene in the church (IV.i) is matched by the repentance scene in the same church (V.iii). Dogberry's confused questioning of Borachio and Conrade is a mocking reflection of Claudio's questioning of Hero. Sometimes devices are repeated, the first occasion as a kind of foreshadowing of the second. Don John makes two attempts to frustrate the wedding; Claudio is twice threatened with a duel, the first perhaps with touches of comedy, the second in earnest. There are antithetical characters: Don John in differing degrees is opposed to the Friar, Don Pedro, and Dogberry.

Fault has been found with some of the characters, particu-larly Claudio, Hero, and Don John. The rejection of Hero has been condemned as brutal, and Beatrice's 'Kill Claudio' has been thought too nearly tragic for a comedy. Yet it is a lively scintillating comedy in which characters strike postures, swallow their words, are hoist with their own petard, deceive others and themselves, eavesdrop, reverse their attitudes, are credulous, lose faith, have faith restored, in short are earnestly and sublimely ridiculous. Benedick sums up himself and all of it, 'For man is a giddy thing, and this is my conclusion'.

Shakespeare's comedies are intended to entertain, but they are not mere farcical froth. Invariably there are judgments of the human condition, 'the very age and body of the time his form and pressure', and loving portrayals of human foibles. Accordingly themes, ideas, notions that give the play its texture and colour have been noted. Variously it is a play about knowing, about mis-noting, about honour; about appearance and reality, fancy and true love, credulity and self-deception. It is a comedy of masks, it is made up of 'misapprehensions, misprisions, misunderstandings, misinterpretations and misapplications' (Rossiter). It is about the triumph of love over hate – Don Pedro, the maker of marriages, over Don John, the breaker of marriage – in keeping with a tradition in which love and hate are personified as brothers and so portrayed in Spenser's *Faerie Queene* (IV.x.32). Shakespeare uses the notion again in *The Tempest*, *As You Like It*, and *King Lear*. It is a quest for love's truth (J. R. Brown); it is concerned with the sanctity of marriage. R. G. Hunter describes it as a comedy of forgiveness in the tradition of the morality and miracle plays, where a human being sins, repents, is forgiven. The essential point is forgiveness and hope of salvation, not the meting out of rewards and punishments. His claim has support from the sacramental tones of Claudio's repentance and of the monument scene.

Some of Shakespeare's audience may have seen in the characters traces of personified virtues and vices: Hero (Truth, Innocence), Claudio (Youth, Repentance), Don John (Envy, Calumny), Dogberry (Justice), Leonato (Father

Time). Then, following a hint in Don Pedro's words, 'as time shall try' (I.i.231), we may see the romantic plot as a dramatic representation of a proverb extensively personified in emblem, pageant, picture, poetry, and by Shakespeare on at least seven occasions. 'Time's glory is ... To unmask falsehood and bring truth to light' (*Lucrece*, 939–40). There are many versions. Time is a justice who tries all offenders, Time is the father of Truth, Time rescues Truth from Calumny, and from concealment, Time unveils Truth.

IV

CLAUDIO

Critics have little good to say of Claudio. Cold, callous, brash, mercenary are some of the terms used. Surely with unnecessary harshness he is said to be, 'more likely to ravish a heroine than be speechless'. He lusts after Hero's body, and will marry her for her fortune – lust and money, Blind Cupid and brothels', seems misconceived. Even his defenders consider him blemished and less than chivalrous in publicly rejecting Hero. It is worth noting at this point that some of the heroes of Shakespeare's comedies are not endearing figures, from the mercenary Bassanio (*Merchant of Venice*) to the 'lascivious boy' Bertram (*All's Well That Ends Well*). They are erring mortals who pass through some kind of trial by humiliation or suffering before they are regenerated, forgiven, and worthy of true love.

Insufficient attention has been paid to Shakespeare's significant characterization of Claudio in the first comments about him. The Messenger announces that Claudio has done the deeds of a lion in the 'figure of a lamb' and the image, even allowing for a rhetorical flourish, is important. It is extended by Don John's jaundiced description, 'A very forward March-chick', a 'young start-up', by Benedick's insulting 'boy', and 'Lord Lackbeard', and by Claudio's attitudes and actions. In short Claudio is an adolescent with an adolescent's contradictory virtues and weaknesses: innocence, inexperience, shrinking sensitivity, idealism, uncertainty, impulsiveness, over-reaction, egotism, inconsiderateness, among others. It may be added that a lamb is proverbially susceptible to the deception of a wolf in sheep's clothing.

He seeks the approval of Benedick to his idealistic view of Hero, but fails to see the value of Benedick's critical judgment. His uncertainty leads him to suspect that Don Pedro's praise of Hero is a trick. So far his love for Hero is tentative and unformed: he would scarcely trust himself not to marry if Hero would be his wife; and if his 'passion change not shortly'. To Elizabethans, as a dependant of Don Pedro, his request for help in his suit would be normal, as would be the matter of Hero's prospective inheritance, the practical side of a marriage and not necessarily what may be understood as an arranged marriage. In his innocence and readiness to believe what he is told, he is a victim of Don John's bland deceit. Not grounded strongly in trust he assumes Don Pedro's disloyalty and shrinks away to suffer in solitude.

Don Pedro's announcement, confirmed by Leonato, that Claudio's marriage to Hero has been agreed stuns Claudio into silence at the sudden overthrow of his suspicions and despair, and the fulfilment of his hopes. Perhaps too, he gazes at Hero in mute rapture that leaves him speechless. It is not necessary to accuse him of dumbness. When Beatrice comically prompts him his words are dignified and gracious.

Faced with Don John's false accusations against Hero he over-reacts, and it is difficult not to regard his action in the church as callous. Some have sought to condone what he does by taking the marriage as an 'arranged marriage', and arguing that he is justifiably outraged by being offered 'damaged goods'. Others consider that the public repudiation of Hero in church is a necessary, powerfully theatrical demonstration of the triumph of Don John's evil plot. Yet Claudio's actions are in keeping with his youth – his sensitivity, immature judgment, and idealism. He reveres Hero and conducts himself blamelessly to achieve an honourable estate of matrimony (IV.i.46–52). The shock of discovering Hero's apparent lechery is severe; deeply hurt, he reacts with wild rage. From his point of view Hero's fault, if true, is heinous. She betrays her bridegroom by taking a lover, of all times on her wedding eve; she shows her contempt for him by playing a parody of their meeting; if she actually intends to go through with the marriage, she will lie in declaring that she knows no impediment to marriage; she will defile the sacrament of marriage; and she will make Claudio, premaritally as it were, a cuckold. In brief, Claudio will be deceived, mocked, cheated, humiliated, and dishonoured – not a small matter.

Claudio's speeches of denunciation are carefully contrived and overlaid with dramatic irony in that the audience is not deceived. Each speech recalls that Hero's beauty and modest bearing indicate her virtue, as in reality they do. These Claudio, bitterly sarcastic, perversely takes as signs of sensuality and lust. Then through classical personifications he generalizes the opposition of virtue and vice but tones down his bitterness. Finally, more gently he laments the pity of it, if only her virtue had matched her outward beauty, and with poignant oxymorons renounces her and love inspired by beauty. This transformation in his feelings from anger to grief and longing and to something approaching compassion raises him in estimation though it leaves him despondent.

When, therefore, Claudio learns of Don John's treachery his immediate admission of error follows naturally: 'Impose me to what penance your invention Can lay upon my sin – yet sinned I not But in mistaking', and Don Pedro offers to 'satisfy this good old man'. The words 'penance', 'sin', 'satisfy' call to mind the sequence, contrition, confession, satisfaction of a repentant sinner seeking forgiveness, undergoing penance, and making amends. This religious tone is increased when Claudio ceremonially places the epitaph on Hero's monument in the church where he had denounced her. Leonato's final penance is to impose on him with a nice touch of irony the marriage that he had first sought and then rejected. In achieving his veiled bride Claudio has learned to be resolute in keeping faith and not to judge by appearances however hideous: 'I'll hold my mind were she an Ethiope'.

His name may be significant. Claudio, Claudius (*Hamlet*), Claudio (*Measure for Measure*) are all impelled to repent. Their name is derived from the Latin root of *claudus*, lame, limping. Beatrice refers to the 'bad legs' of repentance (II.i.66-8) and Spenser in *Faerie Queene*, III.xii.24 describes Repentance in the Masque of Cupid as lame. It would seem that there was some concept or emblem associating lameness with repentance.

V

HERO

Shakespeare's first words describing Hero, 'Is she not a modest young lady' announce her essential qualities of modesty and youthfulness. Modesty to the Elizabethans was shown by bashfulness, silence, and blushing. Brabantio's description of Desdemona illustrates the characteristics: 'A maiden never bold; Of spirit so still and quiet, that her motion Blushed at herself' (*Othello*, I.iii.94-6). In the structure of the play Hero is thus poised as a foil to Beatrice. Like Katharine and Bianca in *The Taming of the Shrew*, 'one as famous for a scolding tongue As is the other for beauteous modesty'. Consequently she has been dismissed as 'passive' and even as 'incredible'. It would be better to regard her as distanced by her modesty and her youthful innocence, and by the romantic picture frame in which she is set. As the heroine of a romantic story she does not initiate action herself, but is one about whom things happen. She is someone to be 'achieved' by a suitable hero after tribulation. Two things about her are emphasized, her truth and her innocence; the former during the church scene and the latter in V.i.

The proxy wooing, the giving of the parental consent, the choosing of the wedding date are features of a fashionable 'arranged' marriage. They are the externals, the appearances of a wedding. It is unlikely that these arrangements are intended to support the notion that Claudio is a fortune-hunter. They more likely demonstrate the unreadiness of bride and groom. After all they have not yet spoken to each other. Even when the announcement is made Hero does not speak openly. They are uncommitted, they have not formed an intimate relationship, heart has not spoken to heart. This point about appearances is perhaps repeated later when Hero discusses her wedding dress with Ursula and Margaret (III.i.101–3; III.iv.6–34).

Some see the Hero of this conversation as shallow, merely interested in clothes, and too squeamish or prudish to face the physical realities of marriage. Such judgments lack perception. The talk of clothes is not unnatural. Her reaction to Margaret's comment 'heavier soon by the weight of a man', far from indicating that Hero refuses to face physical realities, may rather denote her consistent modesty and delicacy in the face of what was a common coarse joke. Moreover, the praise of the 'graceful, and excellent fashion' of Hero's dress underlines her good taste and modesty by comparison with the Duchess of Milan's elaborately decorated dress, a sign of voluptuousness, if not lechery, in the wearer. Dramatically the very lightness of the episode sharpens its irony in view of the impending rejection of Hero. Her feeling of foreboding, a useful reminder to the audience, may also reveal a sensitive awareness that all is not well with the marriage as it is arranged.

With her modesty just affirmed, Hero reacts against Claudio's appalling accusations with restraint. There is no violent expostulation, no fierce counter-attack, but in innocent bewilderment a number of brief simple questions until the intensity of her suppressed emotions causes her to faint.

The Friar's proposals to achieve a 'greater birth. She dying', to cause Claudio to see Hero truly in the 'eye and prospect of his soul', together with Claudio's contrition, penance, and satisfaction, invest Hero with some element of symbolism. It is perhaps not necessary to relate Claudio's change to the Neo-Platonic ladder from sensual love to celestial love as some have suggested. There is more to support the suggestion that Hero's 'death' implies a redemptive sacrifice in view of the use of words with Christian connotations. More simply Leonato's words, 'She died my lord, but whiles her slander lived', point to personifications: Modesty or Truth wounded by Slander, but revived when Slander is exposed, put to flight, and imprisoned. The manner of it is not unlike the sufferings of Una, Truth, in Spenser's *Faerie Queene*. Claudio gains understanding and faith whereby he finally attains to Hero who remains constant throughout like her legendary namesake, a pattern of a true lover.

VI

BEATRICE AND BENEDICK

The 'merry war' between Beatrice and Benedick is perhaps Shakespeare's variation on a proverbial theme, 'the quarrels of lovers are the renewing of love'. It is possible that an earlier love affair from which Benedick retreated and in which Beatrice was hurt (II.i.250–5) may have caused both to adopt defensive postures of hostility to marriage and scorn of the opposite sex. These attitudes they express with vigorous loquacity and barbed wit in startling contrast to the romantic, conventional affair of the tongue-tied Hero and Claudio. Consequently to others they appear unfashionable and perverse (III.i.72–3).

It is often held that their course in the play is a journey of self-discovery aided by the deception of friends and the shock of the accusation against Hero. Yet signs of interest in each other and in marriage as well as of self-discovery occur before these episodes. At the outset Beatrice's mocking requests for news of Benedick and her deprecatory account of him denote her involvement with him, and even a hint of possessiveness. Are her remarks framed to discover the truth about Benedick, or, to gratify her by hearing her slanders refuted and Benedick praised, or, to demonstrate her superiority over him? In other words is he a sham Hercules, all verbiage and no valour? Is he a fashionable carpet knight, inconstant in friendship and a sponger? The knowledge is important since Benedick is a necessity for her. He is the only one in the play with whom she can communicate on equal terms, he enhances her wit, her essential quality. The others are her stooges. She finds it necessary to apologize to Don Pedro for exercising her wit at his expense (II.i.297–8); she is condescending in her advice to Hero (II.i.45–8); scathing to Margaret (III.iv.41–3, 60–1) – who it must be admitted gives as good as she gets – and out-manœuvres Leonato (II.i.19–56). Again, Benedick praises Beatrice's beauty above Hero's (I.i.170–2); he contemplates the possibility of marriage (II.iii.19–20); and marriage to Beatrice was at least in his mind though he rejects it (II.i.226–8). Beatrice, too, though she rejects the notion of a husband, bearded or beardless (II.i.24–34), yet complains that everyone is getting married while she may sit in a corner and cry 'Heigh-ho for a husband' (II.i.288–9).

The apophthegm, 'Man's love is of man's life a thing apart, 'Tis woman's whole existence', is applicable to the attitudes of Benedick and Beatrice. Benedick's pose of hostility to love and marriage on the grounds that he does not wish to be cuckolded is put on rather like a garment. Its sincerity is put in doubt by the ribaldry it attracts and his too-much protesting. He himself enquires of Claudio, 'would you have me speak after my custom, as being a professed tyrant to their sex?', or, with my 'simple true judgment?', admitting the pose. Claudio later confirms this pose by observing of Benedick, 'And never could maintain his part but in the force of his will'. Consequently, in view of Claudio's conversion from soldier to lover, Benedick considers whether he too may not succumb, and argues himself into a receptive mood. After hearing the plotters, his reflections move from self-criticism, self-approval, self-determination to a discarding of his former custom – 'I will be horribly in love with her'. He supports his intention by comic altruism – 'the world must be peopled', and a former declaration he stands on its head – 'I did not think I should live till I were married'. The process appears to owe more to gymnastics of the mind than to throbs of the heart.

There is no indication that Beatrice similarly discards a pose, only that she will shed her disdain and humble her pride. She is more intense than Benedick. Her shrewishness is an exaggeration of an innate quality. Her intention not to marry is not taken too seriously by the others, who yet warn her that she may succeed in not getting a husband. She has real doubts about the manly qualities of her suitors. Her defence is 'maiden pride' and scorn. Hero fiercely attacks these: 'Disdain and scorn ride sparkling in her eyes, Misprizing what they look on', and again, 'She cannot love, Nor take no shape nor project of affection, She is so self-endeared'. There is no comedy attached to her eavesdropping, no comment from her until her sincere, simple soliloquy acknowledging her faults and announcing her loving response.

The differences are reflected in the nature of their wit. Beatrice, born under a star that danced, and, 'to speak all mirth and no matter', has a swift, trenchant wit that deals with meanings. Benedick's wit is more expansive, fertile with invention, and genial comedy keeps breaking in. His wit is more playful, inviting the listeners to share it with him. Beatrice's sharp mind gives no quarter. Benedick's comment on her wordplay, 'Thou hast frighted the word out of his right sense, so forcible is thy wit', is apt for she overpowers him. At their first encounter he gives up with a 'jade's trick'; in the masking scene his disguise makes it impossible for him to defend himself; and later in the same scene he flees in mock horror from her who 'speaks poniards, and every word stabs'.

When their eavesdropping scenes are over, both are bemused. Benedick, the realist as far as Claudio is concerned, gives way to ludicrous fancies. Later, his excuse of the toothache shows a deplorable lack of invention, while Beatrice clumsily assumes a cold and is notably imperceptive about *Carduus Benedictus*.

The shock of Hero's apparent disgrace and rejection sweeps away the indulgence of wit and the barriers of pretence. Beatrice's passionate loyalty to Hero and her sense of outrage, face Benedick with the reality of love. Her demand of him, 'Kill Claudio', challenges him to prove his love at the expense of his friend. There is some irony in the topsy-turvy attitudes they now find themselves supporting: Beatrice demands the death of Claudio for rejecting a marriage, and Benedick is prepared to risk his life for a woman apparently guilty of pre-marital cuckolding of her bridegroom.

When they meet again there is urbanity and playfulness in their banter. They tease each other from a position of security and mutual trust. Benedick, who after all has been mocked more than anyone else in the play, restores his own good conceit of himself. Since no one else would do it for him, he bears witness to his own praiseworthiness and becomes trumpet to his own virtues. Even the admission of those who plotted to bring them together does not disturb them.

Both names signify blessedness. Perhaps Shakespeare with a nice touch of irony linked their denunciation of marriage as qualifying them for that 'single blessedness' that Hermia (*A Midsummer Night's Dream*, I.i.78) vowed to follow rather than marry Demetrius, and which St Paul preferred (*I Cor.*, vii.1). In their marriage not only are they blessed sacramentally, but ironically loving 'no more than reason' they fuse reason and love in blessed harmony. Bottom, who lamented 'reason and love keep little company together now-a-days', would have approved the successful plotting of their 'honest neighbours'.

VII

DOGBERRY AND THE WATCH

The activities of the Watch comment ironically on the antics of the major characters in the play. With single-minded complacency they present comic antitheses that put in a gentler perspective the villainies of Don John, and soften the asperities of the rejection scene.

There is a perverse logic about Dogberry's insistence that the Watch must refrain from carrying out their duties lest they should give offence, and this is neatly in keeping with his words that express the opposite of what he intends. The Watch's duty is to arrest offenders, if the Watch give offence to anyone, they are themselves offenders. Confidently he answers their questions, step by step denuding the Watch of its proper functions. Even sleeping on watch he approves as without offence. His offer to bet on his knowledge of the statutes is a piece of triumphant one-upmanship. Equally perverse is Don John's determination to give offence. Contrary to Dogberry's policy of inoffensive inactivity, he seeks 'any model to build mischief on', and, 'to despite them I will endeavour anything'. It is neatly ironical that the Watch discover and arrest the villains, the fools defeat the knaves, and even more that the wrong charge is preferred against them.

While Beatrice spells her victims backward, Dogberry presents his meanings backward. His verbal topsy-turvy-dom is a mocking echo of the verbal brilliance of Beatrice and Benedick. Not that Dogberry is without wit. He answers the questions of his followers with unusual clarity and with a deft quibble – 'they are not the men you took them for', and, 'let him … steal out of your company'. His magnificently disordered *partitio* (V.i.203–7) in its own way reflects Beatrice's fierce attack on Claudio and Don Pedro, the details are essentially the same. These two, like Borachio and Conrade, are 'both in a tale'.

There are interesting parallels between the Friar and Dogberry. Both are counsellors, leaders, and acquainted with books. Even though the 'learned Constable is too cunning to be understood', through him the truth comes to light. His initial stating of a conviction of guilt before the evidence is heard, though ratified by the Sexton and the subsequent eliciting of the truth, is a more wholesome affair than the narrow prejudice that condemns Hero of guilt.

For Dogberry himself his self-delusion, complacency, and pomposity preserve him from deflation, though his dignity is outraged by his being called an ass – the taunt lingers. He claims to 'spare for no wit', yet in excitement he commits verbal excesses and rambling inconsequences. In spite of his malapropisms which are rather mirror-meaning words than true malapropisms, the intended meaning comes through. He condescends to Verges, though he has a warm affection for him. He treats Leonato variably – now with respect, now on terms of equality, now as a boy, patronizingly. Finally, in an ecstasy of thankfulness for his success, for the approval he has gained, and for the largess bestowed on him, he invokes a largess of God's blessings on all around: disconcerting 'God save the foundation', and a final exit negative, 'if a merry meeting may be wished, God prohibit it'!

VIII

DON JOHN

For Elizabethans Don John's bastardy would at once announce his disposition. Illegitimate children were the consequence of flouting law, custom, and order. Bastard sons were therefore legally barred from inheritance, and excluded from society's amenities in other ways. It was held that bastards were deformed and tainted in mind by the sin of their begetting, so that they inherited more of the sin that all inherit after the Fall from Eden. As B. G. Lyons expresses it ... 'bastards were living emblems of their parents' sin in begetting them'. Disadvantaged in society and more prone to sin, bastards were marked by melancholy, envy, and malice.

Don John declares that he is a 'plain-dealing villain', a device used by Shakespeare to announce such villains as Edmund (*King Lear*), Iago (*Othello*), and Richard III. He refuses to 'hear reason' and asserts that he will do as he pleases. This establishes that his corrupt will has overpowered the divine quality of reason in him. He rejects brotherly love and grace, and reveals his obsession with the deadly sin of envy by likening himself to its symbol, the dog (I.iii.30, 32). Born out of wedlock he is the enemy of marriage. He is both the agent of evil and a scapegoat for it in that he frees others from the ultimate blame.

IX

THEMES

Proverbially appearances are deceptive, and in *Much Ado About Nothing* which is mainly constructed out of deceptions the reality or truth behind appearances is constantly in question.

Claudio, attracted by Hero's appearance, assumes that she is modest (I.i.147), 'the sweetest lady that ever I looked on' (I.i.167–8), in spite of Benedick's doubts about the inference. Under the stress of Don John's lie, Claudio now regards her beauty as 'a witch Against whose charms faith melteth into blood' (II.i.161–2). Borachio's plot to make 'appear such seeming truth of Hero's disloyalty' (II.ii.43) is so effective that even her facial expressions of modesty and innocence Claudio interprets as signs of guilt. Her unfortunate phrase, 'seemed I ever otherwise', enrages him to a tirade against 'seeming', and later, a bitter lament on the paradox of fair appearance and foul reality (IV.i.99–106). The Friar, out of his observation and experience, interprets rightly the significance of the 'blushing apparitions' and 'innocent shames' on Hero's face. He hopes that the plan he propounds will cause Hero to appear in a true light in the eye of Claudio's soul (IV.i.227). After his repentance Claudio is resolute in discarding mere outward appearance: 'I'll hold my mind were she an Ethiope' (V.iv.38).

Beatrice and Benedick out of their self-deception have erected each a façade from which they conduct their merry war, itself a paradox, an appearance without reality. When Benedick eavesdrops on those who are deceiving him he is convinced that it is no trick because the conference appeared to be seriously ('sadly') conducted, and included the white-bearded Leonato: 'knavery cannot sure hide himself in such reverence' (II.iii.116–17).

Dogberry and the Watch are prime self-deceivers. Outwardly armed with the authority and dignity of the law, they should be vigilant to maintain order and to arrest offenders; in truth they propose to let offenders steal out of their company, and to sleep when they should be awake.

Another aspect of appearance is fashion. The word in its variant forms and senses occurs more frequently in *Much Ado About Nothing* than in any other of Shakespeare's plays. Borachio's account of fashion, 'Seest thou not, I say, what a deformed thief this fashion is, how giddily 'a turns about all the hot bloods between fourteen and five-and-thirty' (III.iii.125–7) makes the points of its deception and inconstancy. The 'deformed thief' fashion 'goes up and down like a gentleman' (III.iii.121–2); 'fashion-monging boys' assume 'outward hideousness' (V.i.94–6). Preoccupation with fashion indicates interest in appearances only. Claudio carves the fashion of a new doublet (II.iii.16); Hero debates the fashion of her rebato, tire, and wedding dress. Fashion as a verb sometimes carries implications of plotting and intrigue, of contriving appearances. Borachio 'will so fashion' trouble for Hero (II.ii.41–2); Don Pedro hopes to fashion a match (II.i.334); the Friar hopes that success will fashion the event in better shape (IV.i.233). The Friar apart, fashion in the play is a deceitful and corrupting element.

Beatrice accuses Benedick of inconstancy: 'he wears his faith but as the fashion of his hat; it ever changes with the next block' (I.i.65–6). Faith here is placed in opposition to fashion; it is a theme that permeates the play. Claudio temporarily loses faith in Don Pedro who, he believes, has broken faith with him in the wooing of Hero: 'for beauty is a witch Against whose charms faith melteth into blood' (II.i.161–2). After witnessing Borachio and Margaret at Hero's window he loses faith in her as does Don Pedro. The Friar, by virtue of his calling almost a symbol of faith, maintains his belief in Hero's innocence. Beatrice passionate in her faith in Hero rouses Benedick to pledge his love and faith, if necessary, to death.

A complementary theme of 'knowing' has been pointed out. The word and its variant forms occur with great frequency. Some consider that the title contains the pun 'nothing' – 'noting' both then pronounced 'noting'. 'Note' and 'know' are doublets. R. Berry, *Shakespeare's Comedies* (1972) defines situations in the play as those arising from intrigue, from chance, and from inference. Each of the situations presents knowledge upon which characters act whether the knowledge is true or false. He goes further and suggests that '"Know" is the conceptual principle of the play'.

Music in performance and by allusion forms a pattern in the structure of the play. Some, in the light of Don Pedro's quibble on 'nothing' (II.iii.53), have argued that there is a similar musical quibble in the title of the play. It was held that order and harmony in the universe and in man were created and maintained by love and made manifest by the music of the spheres and in man by music and dancing.

At the beginning of the play music is linked with the introduction of a love theme (I.ii.11–12, 21–3), music and dancing in a masque provide the occasion for the proxy wooing of Hero by Don Pedro, and Don Pedro announces the success of his wooing on Claudio's behalf, when accused by Benedick of stealing the 'bird's nest', by declaring, 'I will but teach them to sing, and restore them to the owner' (II.i.209–10).

Balthasar's excuses for his bad voice and fear that he may 'slander music', and Benedick's wish that Balthasar's 'bad voice bode no mischief', are reminders of the deceit about to be practised on Benedick. The advice given in the song to love-lorn ladies prefigures the conspirators' account of Beatrice's alleged sufferings and the advice they give her.

Benedick in his despising of love and marriage regards love

as the subject of disreputable ballads (I.i.223–4), condemns Claudio's change of interest from acceptable martial music to the inferior tabor and pipe, and, associating marriage with cuckoldry, declares with ominous double meaning a preference for, 'a horn for my money' (II.iii.54–7). His conversion to love is still incomplete when he fails to compose a love song.

Beatrice, too, sees wooing and marriage as a deterioration in harmony to the final pathetic cinquepace into the grave (II.i.67–8).

Don John, the enemy of love and harmony, rejects music (I.iii.31) and does not appear to join in the dancing (II.i.138ff). Perhaps the absence of music leading to Hero's wedding and the omission of the serenade (though this may be done to avoid confusing the audience) are consistent with the disruption. For certainly music might have been expected at the wedding ceremony.

The solemn music and the dirge by the monument (V.iii) is in effect atonement and a plea for reconciliation and harmony. The final reconciliation and restoration of harmony are celebrated by music and dancing.

X

WORDPLAY

The Elizabethan grammar schools included rhetoric in their curriculum. This was an elaborate system of word devices whereby a speaker could impress, persuade, and convince his audience. While Shakespeare makes extensive use of such devices in the dialogue of Beatrice and Benedick, they are also prominent in the Messenger's announcement in I.i.12–16 and in Dogberry's incoherences. Here are a few devices, apart from metaphor, commonly used by Shakespeare.

The witty exchanges of Beatrice and Benedick rely very

much on the pun. So vigorously does Beatrice employ the device that Benedick protests, 'Thou hast frighted the word out of his right sense, so forcible is thy wit' (V.ii.51–2). The pun was not regarded as the lowest form of wit, it had the authority of the Bible and classical writers. It could be an elegant deployment of wit, or an expression of a wide range of emotions from jest to hysteria, or a means of shifting the ground in a pseudo-logical 'proof', or the mainspring of a sequence of images. The Elizabethans distinguished four kinds: a word repeated with a different meaning – 'kind', 'kindness' (I.i.25), 'Note', 'notes' (II.iii.50–3), 'protest' (IV.i.275–83); a word bearing different meanings at the same time – 'wit' (III.i.76), 'stomach' (I.i.46); words repeated or alluded to which are similar in sound – 'civil' (II.i.265), 'barns' (III.iv.43); a word repeated, often as a retort, with an unexpected change of meaning – 'get', 'getting' (II.i.290–1), 'seemed', 'seeming' (IV.i.53–4). But, as Mahood points out in her *Shakespeare's Wordplay*, Shakespeare's imagination works through puns as a poet, dramatist, and dramatic poet, and not as a mere follower of rhetorical rules.

By contrast, another device used by Shakespeare particularly to sharpen the anguish of a mind struggling between conflicting emotions, or to emphasize a truth, is oxymoron, the placing together of two words of opposite meaning. Don John's bitter irony is sharpened by 'plain-dealing villain' (I.iii.29). Claudio cries out 'Thou pure impiety and impious purity' (IV.i.102). Incidentally this phrase exemplifies another device, antimetabole or chiasmus, the inversion of the order of repeated words to emphasize the meaning or mark a contrast – 'to weep at joy than to joy at weeping' (I.i.27). Contrasting ideas are often emphasized by balanced antitheses – 'doing in the figure of a lamb the feats of a lion' (I.i.14–15), 'I cannot be a man with wishing, therefore I will die a woman with grieving' (IV.i.316–18); or expressive of irony and

23

sarcasm – 'enfranchised with a clog' (I.iii.30); or denoting
mental confusion – suffer salvation' (III.iii.2–3). Repetition of
a word or phrase is often used to produce a climax, or anticlimax. Benedick is an exponent of this – 'too' (I.i.153–4),
'that' (I.i.212–14), 'yet' (II.iii.24–5).

These devices and many more should not be considered in
isolation from their dramatic integration with situation, emotion, or action.

XI

VERSE AND PROSE

Verse in the play is subdued and at times almost pedestrian.
It has none of the elaboration and richness to be found in· *The
Merchant of Venice*, or in the varied rhyming patterns of *Love's
Labour's Lost*. Apart from Balthasar's Song (II.iii.58) and the
Epitaph and Dirge where rhyme is natural, there is very little
of it elsewhere. After overhearing Hero and Ursula, Beatrice's heartfelt resolve is sealed as it were in two quatrains
with alternate rhymes and a final couplet (III.i.107–16). The
ritual of the monument scene with its Epitaph and Dirge is
maintained to the end by ten lines rhyming alternately. The
Friar confirms his advice with a quatrain (IV.i.249–52);
couplets point the repartee between Claudio and Benedick
(V.iv.46–51). Couplets marking exits are rare.

Blank verse is the medium in which the affairs of Hero are
presented. Except for the conversation with her ladies on the
morning of her wedding, Hero herself speaks in blank verse,
even when deceiving the eavesdropping Beatrice. Don Pedro,
Claudio, and Benedick in IV.i, all use blank verse when refer-
ring to Hero. Later, Benedick deviates into verse on his own
account (V.ii.25–8). On the whole the blank verse is undist-
inguished. What Beatrice overhears is fluent narrative with
simple similes and comparisons. In the denunciation scene

24

Claudio's condemnation of Hero is spoken more in sorrow than in agony. It has not the tortured turbulence of Othello. The Friar's advice is good staple verse, flexible and lucid. Leonato's lament (V.i.3–38) has convincing sincerity and power, telling images and aphorisms.

It may be that Shakespeare restrained the emotional aspects of the Claudio–Hero plot in this way lest it should get out of hand and veer the play away from comedy to tragedy. Or again, he may have wished to maintain it in a steadfast course to happiness by contrast with the eccentric shifts of Benedick and Beatrice.

The range of prose is considerable. The Messenger presents his message with a formal flourish of alliteration, parallel phrases, puns, and a paradox. Leonato's courteous reply elegantly uses the same kind of pun, and sums up the paradox with an antimetabole. After these rhetorical courtesies the prose reⅼaxes as Beatrice mounts her onslaught against Benedick, and twists the bewildered Messenger's praises of him into detractions. When Benedick arrives, there is a passage of verbal thrust and counter-thrust between them, each nimbly quibbling or distorting the other's words in an odd kind of antiphon. Benedick, left with Claudio, reverts briefly to a conversational style. Then, expressing his views on Hero's modesty and the unworthiness of women, he orders his thoughts in parallel steps to a climax, or even an anticlimax, and a piece of specious logic. All this variety occurs in the first scene.

Both Beatrice and Benedick express themselves with a fertility of invention and flexibility of syntax not found in the other characters. Up to the bower scene Beatrice brilliantly deploys her wit. She reduces a proverb by extending its argument (II.i.19–21), demolishes a suggestion by neatly shifting ground in a reply that is logical in form but not in meaning (II.i.30–4), counters one popular belief by another, its opposite (II.i.34–40), produces a pun to prove the impossibility of marrying any man (II.i.51), and sets out, with analogies from dancing, the decline of marriage (II.i.60–8). She again plays on the word to characterize Claudio, 'civil count, civil as an orange' (II.i.265), and outrageously to Don Pedro, 'I would rather have one of your father's getting' (II.i.291). Throughout she employs more puns and quibbles than Benedick.

In the same scene Benedick's prose, particularly II.i.169–247, stresses his anxiety with its lively similes, comparisons, metaphors, extravagant allusions in a style more discursive and narrative than his previous prose. It is freer too from elaborate rhetorical schemes. In his soliloquy at the beginning of II.iii he reflects on the changes in Claudio in parallel sentences depicting Claudio then and now. Considering the possibility that he too may fall in love, he lists the prospective bride's qualities in balanced sentences leading to a flippant anticlimax. His soliloquy at the end of the scene with its brief sentences signals rapid changes of thought, a rush of new notions, and justifications for his change of attitude – all giving the air of improvisations.

The two confess their love (IV.i.264–83) in simple and plain style. Beatrice, however, breaks out with passionate exclamations and cumulative epithets of denunciation against Claudio and Don Pedro.

Benedick continues to speak directly in challenging Claudio, but when he and Beatrice meet again (V.ii.40ff) they resume their wordplay. This time Benedick's protest is milder, 'Thou hast frighted the word out of his right sense, so forcible is thy wit' (V.ii.51–2).

Don John's isolation from the other main characters and his self-interest are reflected in the rhetorical structures of his first speeches as well as in their content (I.iii.10–17, 25–34). The closely parallel sentences, the comparisons, antitheses, concessives, and imagery all stress the repeated 'I'. Later, in slandering Hero (III.ii.98–110) he is given plain prose free from devices, with short effective sentences, and almost casual conditional clauses as if to suggest his disinterestedness.

In spite of his malapropisms and inversions of meaning, Dogberry's speeches manage to convey the correct thought. Exceptionally his answers to the watchmen's questions are clearly stated and free from misused words, though he does rely on two puns to maintain his omniscience. His style is colloquial, interrupted by such interjections as 'marry', 'truly', 'why', 'in faith', and by invocations to God. He supports his views with proverbs and everyday sayings that are not always relevant. His assessment of the villains (V.i.203–7) in the form of a *partitio* is the high point of his rhetoric and of his function as a constable.

Borachio may believe that he tells his 'tale vilely' (III.iii.140–1), but there is nothing incoherent in the structure of his sentences. His similes are certainly unusual, and the sequence of his story is disordered, but Shakespeare has taken pains to see that the audience is in no doubt what has happened.

MUCH ADO ABOUT NOTHING

CHARACTERS

DON PEDRO, Prince of Arragon
DON JOHN, his bastard brother
CLAUDIO, a young lord of Florence
BENEDICK, a young lord of Padua
LEONATO, Governor of Messina
ANTONIO, his brother
BORACHIO ⎫
CONRADE ⎭ followers of Don John
BALTHASAR, a singer
FRIAR FRANCIS
DOGBERRY, a constable
VERGES, a headborough
A SEXTON
A BOY
HERO, Leonato's daughter
BEATRICE, Leonato's niece
MARGARET ⎫
URSULA   ⎭ Gentlewomen attendant on Hero
Messengers, Watch, Attendants

SCENE: *Messina*

Acts, scenes, and locations are not marked in Q; they have been added by editors. Locations can sometimes be inferred from the text.

Suggest an appropriate location. (See ll. 83–5, 142, 182–3, I.ii.8–9 and I.iii.53–5.)

S.D.   *Messenger.* He should be distinguished from the others by riding dress and cloak, etc.
       Leonato should have a white beard. (See II.iii.116.)
1   *Don Pedro.* See Appendix I.
2   *Messina.* A town in Sicily.
3–4   *three leagues*, nine miles.
6   *action*, battle.
7   *sort*, class. *none of name*, no gentlemen. Some take 'name' to mean 'distinction', but this does not agree with Leonato's question and reply. See *Henry V*, IV.viii.98.
8–9   *A ... numbers.* Proverbial.
10   *honour*, i.e. praise, rewards, or titles.
10–16 *young ... how.* Here and in ll. 69–72 Claudio's youthfulness is made clear.
12–13 *equally remembered*, correspondingly rewarded.
14   *figure*, (a) imagined shape, (b) emblem, (c) likeness.
14–15 *in ... lion.* Proverbially 'in peace a lamb, in war a lion'. Balanced antithesis is marked by alliteration.
15–16 *He ... how.* The rhetorical figures of repetition strain the sentence but reinforce the main notion, 'bettered expectation'.
       Is the Messenger – pompous, affected, pleased with himself, straining after an impressive style?
17   *uncle.* Not mentioned again.
20–2   *even ... bitterness.* Proverbially 'no joy without sorrow'. Joy, it was supposed, caused a sudden expansion of the spirits from the heart, and this, if excessive, forced out tears from the brain.

21   *modest*, humble, moderate, decorous.
21–2   *badge of bitterness*, sign of sorrow, tears.

ACT ONE

SCENE ONE

Enter LEONATO, *Governor of Messina,* HERO, *his daughter,* BEATRICE, *his niece, with a Messenger*

LEONATO: I learn in this letter that Don Pedro of Arragon comes this night to Messina.

MESSENGER: He is very near by this; he was not three leagues off when I left him.

LEONATO: How many gentlemen have you lost in this action?

MESSENGER: But few of any sort and none of name.

LEONATO: A victory is twice itself when the achiever brings home full numbers. I find here that Don Pedro hath bestowed much honour on a young Florentine called Claudio. 11

MESSENGER: Much deserved on his part and equally remembered by Don Pedro. He hath borne himself beyond the promise of his age, doing in the figure of a lamb the feats of a lion. He hath indeed better bettered expectation than you must expect of me to tell you how.

LEONATO: He hath an uncle here in Messina will be very much glad of it.

MESSENGER: I have already delivered him letters, and there appears much joy in him; even so much that joy could not show itself modest enough without a badge of bitterness. 22

LEONATO: Did he break out into tears?

25   *kind*, (a) natural, (b) affectionate. *kindness*, (a) kinship, (b) affection.

25-6   *no . . . washed*. The face was regarded as an index of character. Here
       there is a glance at faces made-up with cosmetics and so false.

27   *to . . . weeping*. A rhetorical figure called antimetabole. Leonato's
       reply is in a similar rhetorical mode to that of the Messenger. Is
       he courteous or ironic?

28   *Signor Mountanto*, Sir Stuck-up. *Mountanto*, up-thrust in fencing.
       Perhaps Beatrice implies that Benedick is a conceited opponent
       in wit contests.

31   *sort*, rank.

34   *pleasant*, witty, facetious.

35-6   *He . . . flight*, he posted up notices challenging Cupid to an archery
       match, i.e. that he would make more ladies languish for love than
       Cupid's arrows could do.

36   *flight*, (a) long-distance shooting, (b) flight of the quarry in fal-
       conry, (c) 'flyte', contest.

37-8   *subscribed . . . bird-bolt*, i.e. signed below as for Cupid and chose
       bird-bolts as his weapons.

38   *bird-bolt*, (a) blunt arrow used for shooting at birds, (b) used in
       pranks by fools. Perhaps there is a quibble on 'bird' = girl. See
       Cymbeline, IV.ii.197.

39-40 *But . . . . killing*. According to Beatrice's comments so far, Bene-
       dick is boastful, swaggering, conceited, easily outwitted, deflated
       by the fool, ladies' man. Cf. the comment on the boastful Dau-
       phin, 'I think he will eat all he kills' (*Henry V*, III.vii.86).

41   *tax*, find fault with.

42   *meet*, even.

44-5   *You . . . it*. Beatrice plays on 'service', (a) waiting at table, (b) food
       served, and perhaps 'meet', meat.

44   *holp*, helped.

45   *valiant trencher-man*, (a) hearty eater, (b) brave slasher (swords-
       man). In *Love's Labour's Lost*, V.ii.464, 'trencher-knight' = good at
       feasting not at fighting.

45-6   *excellent stomach*, (a) unequalled courage, (b) hearty appetite.

48   *soldier . . . lady*, i.e. more active in the boudoir than on the battle-
       field. Amourousness and gluttony were taken to be yoke-mates.
       to, to, (a) in attendance on, (b) compared with.

50   *stuffed with*, full of, endowed with.

52   *stuffed man*, dummy figure.

MESSENGER: In great measure.

LEONATO: A kind of overflow of kindness; there are no faces truer than those that are so washed. How much better is it to weep at joy than to joy at weeping.

BEATRICE: I pray you, is Signor Mountanto returned from the wars or no?

MESSENGER: I know none of that name, lady; there was none such in the army of any sort.   31

LEONATO: What is he that you ask for, niece?

HERO: My cousin means Signor Benedick of Padua.

MESSENGER: O he's returned, and as pleasant as ever he was.

BEATRICE: He set up his bills here in Messina, and challenged Cupid at the flight; and my uncle's fool, reading the challenge, subscribed for Cupid, and challenged him at the bird-bolt. I pray you, how many hath he killed and eaten in these wars? But how many hath he killed? For indeed I promised to eat all of his killing.   40

LEONATO: Faith niece you tax Signor Benedick too much; but he'll be meet with you, I doubt it not.

MESSENGER: He hath done good service, lady, in these wars.

BEATRICE: You had musty victual and he hath holp to eat it; he is a very valiant trencher-man, he hath an excellent stomach.

MESSENGER: And a good soldier too, lady.

BEATRICE: And a good soldier to a lady. But what is he to a lord?

MESSENGER: A lord to a lord, a man to a man, stuffed with all honourable virtues.   51

BEATRICE: It is so indeed, he is no less than a stuffed man; but for the stuffing – well, we are all mortal.

54-6 *You ... them.* Is the Messenger – bewildered, stuffy, indignant, out of his depth, dim-witted, dignified, annoyed?

55 *merry war.* What relationship does this imply?

58 *five wits.* Five faculties of the mind which were supposed to correspond with the five senses. They were imagination, memory, fantasy, judgment, common sense, the last being the faculty that combined the evidence from the senses. *halting,* limping.

59-60 *if ... warm,* i.e. if he is wise enough to keep warm, he has the power to reason.

60-2 *let ... creature,* let him display it to distinguish him from his horse, for it is the only valid thing that proves he is a reasoning being.

60 *bear ... difference.* A heraldic expression to describe the inclusion of an alteration to a coat of arms marking a divergence from the main family.

61 *wealth,* possession.

62-3 *companion,* hanger-on.

63 *sworn brother.* Sworn brothers were companions in arms who took an oath by the rules of chivalry to share one another's fortunes, good or bad. Beatrice is ironic.

65 *faith,* i.e. to his sworn brother.

66 *block,* (a) wooden block for shaping or fashioning a felt hat, hence 'fashion', (b) block-head. Rapid changes in gallants' hat-fashions were a matter of ridicule.

67 *books,* favour.

68 *an,* if. *burn my study,* i.e. as containing one inconstant in faith, a heretic.

69 *squarer,* swaggerer.

70 *voyage,* journey.

71-2 *He ... Claudio.* Messenger is pompous and disapproving.

72 *Claudio.* For the possible significance of his name see Introduction. p. 10.

73 *hang upon,* cling to.

74 *pestilence,* plague.

75 *presently,* immediately.

76 *Benedick.* Q, F 'Benedict'. Perhaps a quibble on the name of some disease causing madness. The Benedictine monks were trained in exorcism as part of their rule of life.

76-7 *cost ... cured,* i.e. (a) by extravagance, (b) by Benedick's sponging.

78 *hold,* keep.

80 *run mad,* (a) catch the Benedick, (b) fall in love.

34

LEONATO: You must not, sir, mistake my niece. There is a kind of merry war betwixt Signor Benedick and her; they never meet but there's a skirmish of wit between them.

BEATRICE: Alas he gets nothing by that. In our last conflict four of his five wits went halting off, and now is the whole man governed with one; so that if he have wit enough to keep himself warm, let him bear it for a difference between himself and his horse; for it is all the wealth that he hath left to be known a reasonable creature. Who is his companion now? He hath every month a new sworn brother.

MESSENGER: Is't possible? 64

BEATRICE: Very easily possible: he wears his faith but as the fashion of his hat; it ever changes with the next block.

MESSENGER: I see, lady, the gentleman is not in your books.

BEATRICE: No, an he were, I would burn my study. But I pray you who is his companion? Is there no young squarer now that will make a voyage with him to the devil?

MESSENGER: He is most in the company of the right noble Claudio.

BEATRICE: O Lord, he will hang upon him like a disease; he is sooner caught than the pestilence, and the taker runs presently mad. God help the noble Claudio. If he have caught the Benedick, it will cost him a thousand pound ere 'a be cured.

MESSENGER: I will hold friends with you lady.

BEATRICE: Do, good friend.

LEONATO: You will never run mad niece. 80

BEATRICE: No, not till a hot January.

MESSENGER: Don Pedro is approached.

35

s.d.   A formal entry. How do they greet each other – embrace, curtsey, bow, doff hats, shake hands, kiss, hold hands?

83–4   *are ... trouble?* Proverbially 'he that seeks trouble never misses it'.
84   *trouble*, care and cost.
84–5   *The ... it.* Proverbially 'counting the cost prevents action'. Here Don Pedro quibbles on 'count', 'encounter'.
85   *encounter*, go to meet, confront.
87   *grace*, (a) Grace, (b) graciousness.

90   *charge*, expense, undertaking.

95   *You ... full*, i.e. that thrust went home.
96–7   *fathers herself*, shows who her father is by her likeness to him.
97–8   *Be ... father.* After this speech Don Pedro and Leonato move aside talking.

100   *his head*, i.e. his grey hair and beard.

103   *marks*, listens to.
104   *Lady Disdain.* An emblem figure. It matches Beatrice's name, Signor Mountanto, for Benedick.

107   *meet*, (a) suitable, (b) meat.
108   *convert*, change (faith).
109   *turncoat*, renegade, changer of faith.

111   *find ... heart*, prevail upon myself.
113   *dear happiness*, valuable piece of good fortune. Perhaps a quibble 'dear'/'deer' in view of 'suitor'/'shooter', and on 'heart'/'hart'.

Act One, Scene One

Enter DON PEDRO, CLAUDIO, BENEDICK,
BALTHASAR, *and* DON JOHN *the Bastard*

DON PEDRO: Good Signor Leonato, are you come to meet
your trouble? The fashion of the world is to avoid cost,
and you encounter it.

LEONATO: Never came trouble to my house in the likeness
of your grace. For trouble being gone, comfort should
remain; but when you depart from me, sorrow abides and
happiness takes his leave.

DON PEDRO: You embrace your charge too willingly. I
think this is your daughter.   91

LEONATO: Her mother hath many times told me so.

BENEDICK: Were you in doubt, sir, that you asked her?

LEONATO: Signor Benedick, no, for then were you a child.

DON PEDRO: You have it full, Benedick; we may guess by
this what you are, being a man. Truly the lady fathers
herself. Be happy, lady, for you are like an honourable
father.

BENEDICK: If Signor Leonato be her father, she would not
have his head on her shoulders for all Messina, as like him
as she is.   101

BEATRICE: I wonder that you will still be talking, Signor
Benedick, nobody marks you.

BENEDICK: What, my dear Lady Disdain! Are you yet
living?

BEATRICE: Is it possible disdain should die while she hath
such meet food to feed it as Signor Benedick? Courtesy
itself must convert to disdain, if you come in her presence.

BENEDICK: Then is courtesy a turncoat. But it is certain I
am loved of all ladies, only you excepted; and I would I
could find in my heart that I had not a hard heart, for truly
I love none.   112

BEATRICE: A dear happiness to women; they would else

37

114   *pernicious suitor*, (a) vile suitor, (b) fatal shooter.

115   *I . . . that*, I agree with you in that.

119   *predestinate*, foredoomed, inevitable.

123   *rare parrot-teacher*, fine mimic, i.e. she echoes his words in 'scratch-ing' and 'face'.

124–5   *beast of yours*, i.e. a dumb beast.

126   *I . . . tongue*. Benedick retorts in kind with 'horse' (beast).

129   *You . . . trick*, i.e. refusing to go on like a worn-out horse. Benedick is not 'so good a continuer'.
      Are Beatrice and Benedick – quarrelsome, hostile, playful, affec-tionate, proud, perverse, afraid of each other, on the defensive?

131   *That . . . all*, that concludes our business. Don Pedro and Leonato return to the centre of the stage.

134–6   *he . . . heart*. Apart from the quibble on 'heartily prays' and 'prays from his heart', there is a biblical allusion to the hypocrites con-demned for their insincere praying (*Mark*, vii.6).

140   *I . . . words*. This implies that Don John is a brooding discontented man. Should his dress indicate his isolation?

146   *noted her not*, did not observe her closely.

have been troubled with a pernicious suitor. I thank God and my cold blood, I am of your humour for that. I had rather hear my dog bark at a crow than a man swear he loves me.

BENEDICK: God keep your ladyship still in that mind, so some gentleman or other shall 'scape a predestinate scratched face.   120

BEATRICE: Scratching could not make it worse, an 'twere such a face as yours were.

BENEDICK: Well, you are a rare parrot-teacher.

BEATRICE: A bird of my tongue is better than a beast of yours.

BENEDICK: I would my horse had the speed of your tongue, and so good a continuer. But keep your way a' God's name, I have done.

BEATRICE: You always end with a jade's trick; I know you of old.   130

DON PEDRO: That is the sum of all, Leonato. Signor Claudio and Signor Benedick, my dear friend Leonato hath invited you all. I tell him we shall stay here at the least a month, and he heartily prays some occasion may detain us longer. I dare swear he is no hypocrite, but prays from his heart.

LEONATO: If you swear, my lord, you shall not be forsworn. [*To Don John*] Let me bid you welcome, my lord, being reconciled to the Prince your brother. I owe you all duty.

DON JOHN: I thank you. I am not of many words, but I thank you.   141

LEONATO: Please it your grace lead on?

DON PEDRO: Your hand Leonato; we will go together.
                    [*Exeunt all except Benedick and Claudio*

CLAUDIO: Benedick, didst thou note the daughter of Signor Leonato?

BENEDICK: I noted her not, but I looked on her.

149   *simple*, plain, straightforward.
150   *professed tyrant*, admitted scourge or detractor.

160   *Would . . . her*. Benedick perversely commercializes the discussion.

162   *case*, jewel case.
163   *sad brow*, serious mood. *flouting Jack*, mocking knave.
164–5 *to . . . carpenter*, to tell us that blind Cupid is good at seeing hares
       in their forms, and Vulcan, the god of smiths, is an excellent car-
       penter.
165   *key*, (a) musical mode, (b) attitude of mind.

171   *fury*, spirit of torment.

177   *wear . . . suspicion*, get married, i.e. be under suspicion of wearing
       a cap to hide his cuckold's horns.
178–80 *an . . . Sundays*, i.e. as a prisoner with your yoke-mate sighing in
       repentant prayers.

CLAUDIO: Is she not a modest young lady?

BENEDICK: Do you question me as an honest man should do, for my simple true judgment? Or would you have me speak after my custom, as being a professed tyrant to their sex? 151

CLAUDIO: No, I pray thee speak in sober judgment.

BENEDICK: Why, i'faith, methinks she's too low for a high praise, too brown for a fair praise, and too little for a great praise. Only this commendation I can afford her, that were she other than she is, she were unhandsome; and being no other but as she is, I do not like her.

CLAUDIO: Thou thinkest I am in sport. I pray thee tell me truly how thou likest her.

BENEDICK: Would you buy her, that you inquire after her?

CLAUDIO: Can the world buy such a jewel? 161

BENEDICK: Yea, and a case to put it into. But speak you this with a sad brow? Or do you play the flouting Jack, to tell us Cupid is a good hare-finder, and Vulcan a rare carpenter? Come, in what key shall a man take you to go in the song?

CLAUDIO: In mine eye she is the sweetest lady that ever I looked on.

BENEDICK: I can see yet without spectacles, and I see no such matter. There's her cousin, an she were not possessed with a fury, exceeds her as much in beauty as the first of May doth the last of December. But I hope you have no intent to turn husband, have you? 173

CLAUDIO: I would scarce trust myself, though I had sworn the contrary, if Hero would be my wife.

BENEDICK: Is't come to this? In faith hath not the world one man but he will wear his cap with suspicion? Shall I never see a bachelor of threescore again? Go to i'faith, an thou wilt needs thrust thy neck into a yoke, wear the print

185   *thy allegiance*, your duty to me, your lord.

189   *your grace's part*, what your grace should ask.

191   *If ... uttered*, if I had told him so, this is how he would have
       revealed it.
192-3 *It ... so*. A tale survives in which a girl wanders in a kind of Blue-
       beard's gruesome mansion and sees the bodies of murdered girls.
       Later, she meets and accuses the murderer, and to each of her accu-
       sations he replies, 'It is not so ... so'. Finally a limb and ring are
       produced, and the girl adds 'It is so, and it was so, and here the
       hand I have to show'. His guilt thus proved, the murderer is killed.
       Another jingling expression in the story, 'Be bold, be bold ...
       be not too bold' is used by Spenser in *Faerie Queene*, III.xi.54.
198   *fetch me in*, trick me into admitting it.

201   *by ... troths*, i.e. his allegiance to Don Pedro and to his 'sworn
       brother' Claudio.

205-7 *That ... stake*. Benedick adopts a mock heroic stance of dying for
       his faith like a heretic by fire at the stake.

209   *despite*, despising.
210-11 *And ... will*, and could only keep up this role by perverse wilful-
       ness.

42

of it, and sigh away. Sundays. Look, Don Pedro is returned
to seek you.   181

Enter DON PEDRO

DON PEDRO: What secret hath held you here, that you
followed not to Leonato's?

BENEDICK: I would your grace would constrain me to tell.

DON PEDRO: I charge thee on thy allegiance.

BENEDICK: You hear, Count Claudio. I can be secret as a
dumb man, I would have you think so; but, on my
allegiance, mark you this, on my allegiance – he is in love.
With who? Now that is your grace's part. Mark how short
his answer is: with Hero, Leonato's short daughter.   190

CLAUDIO: If this were so, so were it uttered.

BENEDICK: Like the old tale, my lord: 'It is not so, nor
'twas not so; but indeed, God forbid it should be so.'

CLAUDIO: If my passion change not shortly, God forbid it
should be otherwise.

DON PEDRO: Amen, if you love her; for the lady is very
well worthy.

CLAUDIO: You speak this to fetch me in, my lord.

DON PEDRO: By my troth I speak my thought.

CLAUDIO: And in faith, my lord, I spoke mine.   200

BENEDICK: And by my two faiths and troths, my lord, I
spoke mine.

CLAUDIO: That I love her, I feel.

DON PEDRO: That she is worthy, I know.

BENEDICK: That I neither feel how she should be loved,
nor know how she should be worthy, is the opinion that
fire cannot melt out of me; I will die in it at the stake.

DON PEDRO: Thou wast ever an obstinate heretic in the
despite of beauty.   209

CLAUDIO: And never could maintain his part but in the
force of his will.

43

214–15 *But ... baldrick*, but that I will have a horn on my forehead sounded to summon the hounds, or keep my horn silent and concealed in its sash.

214 *a recheat winded*, a horn call blown.
Benedick will neither openly invite the attention of mocking cynics to his cuckoldry, nor will he conceal it. In short he will not marry and become either a confessed cuckold or one who hides the fact.

218 *fine*, end, conclusion. *finer*, better dressed through having more money.

222–3 *Prove ... drinking*. Sighing with love was supposed to dry up the blood in the heart. Drinking wine proverbially made blood.

223–4 *pick ... pen*. Love, which was 'engendered in the eyes', was a frequent theme of ballads. They were often regarded with contempt because of their scandalous and notorious themes and jingling rhymes.

227 *notable argument*, topic of the day, subject of ridicule.

228–9 *hang ... me*. A cat hung up in a leather basket or bottle was sometimes used as a target in archery.

229–30 *clapped ... shoulder*, hailed with approval.

230 *Adam*, Adam Bell, an outlaw archer famed in ballads.

231 *as ... try*. Proverbial. *try*, prove, put to the test.

232 *In ... yoke*. A reference to a line, 'In time the savage bull sustains the yoke', from Kyd's play, *The Spanish Tragedy* (1587). *savage*, untamed, wild. *yoke*, a shaped wooden bar for coupling oxen drawing a plough.

233 *sensible*, reasonable. Is there perhaps a quibble 'sensi-bull'?

234 *it*, i.e. the marriage yoke.

234–5 *pluck ... forehead*, i.e. as a symbol of a cuckold.

235 *let ... painted*, let a crude picture of me be painted.

237 *signify*, announce.

239–40 *thou ... horn-mad*, you would rage like a bull because your wife was unfaithful.

241–2 *Nay ... shortly*, i.e. Cupid will have his revenge on you for your contempt of love. Benedick has already offended Cupid with his challenge (ll. 35–6), mocked him (ll. 164, 224–5), now Don Pedro warns him (and the audience) that the god will take revenge.

241 *quiver*, case for holding arrows.

242 *Venice*. Notorious for prostitutes in Elizabethan times.

BENEDICK: That a woman conceived me, I thank her; that she brought me up, I likewise give her most humble thanks. But that I will have a recheat winded in my forehead, or hang my bugle in an invisible baldrick, all women shall pardon me. Because I will not do them the wrong to mistrust any, I will do myself the right to trust none. And the fine is, for the which I may go the finer, I will live a bachelor.   219

DON PEDRO: I shall see thee, ere I die, look pale with love.

BENEDICK: With anger, with sickness, or with hunger, my lord; not with love. Prove that ever I lose more blood with love than I will get again with drinking, pick out mine eyes with a ballad-maker's pen, and hang me up at the door of a brothel-house for the sign of blind Cupid.

DON PEDRO: Well, if ever thou dost fall from this faith, thou wilt prove a notable argument.

BENEDICK: If I do, hang me in a bottle like a cat, and shoot at me; and he that hits me, let him be clapped on the shoulder, and called Adam.   230

DON PEDRO: Well, as time shall try:
'In time the savage bull doth bear the yoke.'

BENEDICK: The savage bull may; but if ever the sensible Benedick bear it, pluck off the bull's horns and set them in my forehead; and let me be vilely painted, and in such great letters as they write 'Here is good horse to hire', let them signify under my sign 'Here you may see Benedick the married man.'

CLAUDIO: If this should ever happen, thou wouldst be horn-mad.   240

DON PEDRO: Nay, if Cupid have not spent all his quiver in Venice, thou wilt quake for this shortly.

243   *I ... then*, in that case I shall expect something equally unlikely,
       an earth shaking phenomenon.
244   *temporize ... hours*, conform to time and circumstances (see l. 232).
       Is Benedick hostile to marriage because – he fears being cuckolded,
       it will restrict his freedom, he mistrusts women, he regards falling
       in love with contempt?
245   *repair*, go.
246   *commend me*, give my greetings. *fail him*, fail to attend.
248   *matter*, sense.
249   *and ... you*. Benedick in pompous style is about to call down a
       blessing on them.
250–3 *To ... Benedick*. Claudio and Don Pedro mockingly elaborate his
       'I commit you' into the ending of a letter.
250   *tuition*, care.
254–6 *The ... neither*, the subject of your conversation is sometimes
       decked out with odd phrases that have little to do with it.

256–7 *Ere ... conscience*, before you mock hallowed sayings question the
       rightness of your own motives. *old ends*, (a) fragments of cloth,
       (b) scriptural quotations. See *Richard III*, I.iii.337, 'old odd ends
       stolen out of holy writ'.
259–62 *may ... good*. Note the pattern: 'may do me good ... teach ...
       teach ... how ... how ... learn ... lesson ... may do thee good'.
259   *do me good*, help me.
       Any gesture? See I.iii.55–6.

265   *affect her*, (a) incline towards her, (b) aim at her.

266   *ended action*, war that has just ended.

272   *delicate*, delightful.
273   *prompting*, reminding.

BENEDICK: I look for an earthquake too, then.

DON PEDRO: Well, you will temporize with the hours. In the meantime, good Signor Benedick, repair to Leonato's, commend me to him, and tell him I will not fail him at supper; for indeed he hath made great preparation.

BENEDICK: I have almost matter enough in me for such an embassage; and so I commit you—

CLAUDIO: To the tuition of God. From my house—if I had it—   251

DON PEDRO: The sixth of July. Your loving friend, Benedick.

BENEDICK: Nay, mock not, mock not. The body of your discourse is sometimes guarded with fragments, and the guards are but slightly basted on neither. Ere you flout old ends any further, examine your conscience; and so I leave you.   [*Exit*

CLAUDIO: My liege, your highness now may do me good.

DON PEDRO: My love is thine to teach; teach it but how,
   And thou shalt see how apt it is to learn   261
   Any hard lesson that may do thee good.

CLAUDIO: Hath Leonato any son, my lord?

DON PEDRO: No child but Hero, she's his only heir.
   Dost thou affect her, Claudio?

CLAUDIO: O my lord,
   When you went onward on this ended action,
   I looked upon her with a soldier's eye,
   That liked, but had a rougher task in hand
   Than to drive liking to the name of love.
   But now I am returned, and that war-thoughts   270
   Have left their places vacant, in their rooms
   Come thronging soft and delicate desires,
   All prompting me how fair young Hero is,
   Saying I liked her ere I went to wars.

DON PEDRO: Thou wilt be like a lover presently,

276   *book of words*, volume in her praise.

278–9 *And ... her*. Not in F. Perhaps omitted because of repetition in
      ll. 295–6.

278   *break with*, open the matter, disclose the proposal.

280   *twist ... story*, spin the thread of such an exquisite story.

282   *complexion*, appearance, pallor.

284   *salved*, cleared up, made good. *treatise*, account.
285   *flood*, stream.

286   *The ... necessity*, the best gift fulfils just the need.
287   *Look ... fit*, whatever is sufficient is right. '*Tis once*, once for all.

292   *in her bosom*, to her alone, privately. *unclasp*, open (as a book).
293–4 *And ... tale*, and compel her to listen with the intensity of my
      wooing.
      Is Claudio – immature, sensitive, shy, awkward, mercenary,
      impulsive, uncertain?
      Benedick, mocker and mocked, together with Beatrice's defla-
      tionary wit dominates the scene in contrast to the romantic hero,
      Claudio, naive and easily swayable, and Hero who is silent. There
      is a remarkable display of verbal and other devices: puns, allitera-
      tion, antitheses, slanderous comparisons, false logic, anticlimax,
      antimetabole, parody, hypothetical and fanciful conclusions.
      Themes of fashion, faith, infidelity, seeming, role-playing, noting
      are introduced.

Leonato's house

S.D.   Leonato and Antonio come from different entrances.

1–2   *my ... son*. Appears only in this scene, unless, as some suggest,
      he is Balthasar, the singer.
1   *cousin*, kinsman.
2   *music*, band, orchestra.

And tire the hearer with a book of words.
If thou dost love fair Hero, cherish it;
And I will break with her and with her father,
And thou shalt have her. Was't not to this end
That thou began'st to twist so fine a story?   280
CLAUDIO: How sweetly you do minister to love,
    That know love's grief by his complexion.
    But lest my liking might too sudden seem,
    I would have salved it with a longer treatise.
DON PEDRO: What need the bridge much broader than the
        flood?
    The fairest grant is the necessity.
    Look what will serve is fit. 'Tis once, thou lovest,
    And I will fit thee with the remedy.
    I know we shall have revelling tonight;
    I will assume thy part in some disguise,   290
    And tell fair Hero I am Claudio,
    And in her bosom I'll unclasp my heart,
    And take her hearing prisoner with the force
    And strong encounter of my amorous tale.
    Then after to her father will I break;
    And the conclusion is she shall be thine.
    In practice let us put it presently.   [*Exeunt*

SCENE TWO

Enter LEONATO *and an old man, his brother* ANTONIO

LEONATO: How now brother, where is my cousin your
    son? Hath he provided this music?

4   *strange*, unknown, surprising.

6   *event*, outcome. *stamps*, confirms.

7   *cover*, appearance.

7–12 *The ... dance*. This refers to part of the last speech of Don Pedro to Claudio (I.i.292–5), and implies that the location of I.i. was Antonio's orchard. Leonato and Antonio apparently share the same house. This is the first overhearing that leads to misunderstanding.

8   *thick-pleached*, hedged with intertwined branches. *alley*, walk.

9   *orchard*, garden.

10   *discovered*, revealed.

12   *accordant*, in like mind, sympathetic.

12–13 *take ... top*, seize the immediate opportunity. Proverbially Occasion should be seized by the forelock – the rest of the head is bald and slippery.

14   *wit*, intelligence.

15   *sharp*, alert.

S.D. *Balthasar*, perhaps carrying a lute.

22   *I ... mercy*, I beg your pardon.
       The attitudes of Leonato and Antonio can be distinguished: the one fussy, excited, impatient; the other cautious, prudent, self-controlled.

Leonato's house

Is Don John guarded? As a melancholic malcontent – a notorious Elizabethan type – he may wear significant black, slovenly dress, a hat pulled down over his face, and his gait and speech be slow.

1   *What the good-year*, what the devil! *good-year*. Some kind of evil power. A significantly ominous opening to the scene.

2   *out of measure*, excessively. *sad*, gloomy, melancholy.

3   *measure*, (a) limit, (b) satisfaction. *occasion*, circumstances.

ANTONIO: He is very busy about it. But brother, I can tell you strange news that you yet dreamt not of.

LEONATO: Are they good?

ANTONIO: As the event stamps them, but they have a good cover; they show well outward. The Prince and Count Claudio, walking in a thick-pleached alley in mine orchard, were thus much overheard by a man of mine: the Prince discovered to Claudio that he loved my niece your daughter, and meant to acknowledge it this night in a dance; and if he found her accordant, he meant to take the present time by the top and instantly break with you of it.

LEONATO: Hath the fellow any wit that told you this?

ANTONIO: A good sharp fellow; I will send for him, and question him yourself.

LEONATO: No, no, we will hold it as a dream till it appear itself. But I will acquaint my daughter withal, that she be the better prepared for an answer, if peradventure this be true. Go you and tell her of it.   20

Enter ANTONIO's *son and* BALTHASAR *the musician*

Cousin, you know what you have to do. [*To the musician*] O I cry you mercy friend, go you with me, and I will use your skill. Good cousin have a care this busy time.

[*Exeunt*

SCENE THREE

Enter DON JOHN *the Bastard and* CONRADE *his companion*

CONRADE: What the good-year my lord, why are you thus out of measure sad?

DON JOHN: There is no measure in the occasion that breeds, therefore the sadness is without limit.

6–7   *what ... it*, to the Elizabethan blessings could follow the use of reason. Don John's rejection of his divinely bestowed reason indicates his corrupt nature.

8   *present*, immediate.

9   *sufferance*, endurance.

11   *born under Saturn*. According to astrological beliefs of the time those born under the influence of Saturn, though they could be wise and scholarly, were usually melancholy, deceitful, vengeful, solitary, trouble-makers, and short-lived.

11–12   *moral medicine*, remedy of virtuous conduct.

12   *mortifying mischief*, deadly misfortune, deadening evil plight.

14   *stomach*, appetite.

16–17   *claw ... humour*, flatter no man's whim, humour no man.

16   *claw*, stroke.

19   *controlment*, restraint, curb. Don John proclaims his self-centred nature with the repeated 'I' in this speech and in ll. 25–34.

20   *stood out against*, rebelled against. In the source story Don Pedro had just defeated an attempt by his brother to take the kingdom from him.

22–4   *take ... harvest*. The image of growing plant-like in someone's favour is common in Shakespeare. See *Macbeth*, I.iv.29.

23   *frame the season*, make your opportunity, prepare the climate. *season*, (a) time, opportunity, (b) climate.

25   *canker*, dog-rose.

26   *grace*. ? quibble on 'grass'. *blood*, (a) temperament, (b) lineage as illegitimate, (c) noble birth.

27   *fashion a carriage*, assume a demeanour. *rob*, win.

28–9   *I ... villain*. Declaration by a villain of his character is a device used frequently by Shakespeare, e.g. Edmund (*King Lear*), Iago (*Othello*), Richard (*Richard III*). *flattering ... villain*. Oxymorons and antitheses.

29–30   *I...clog*, i.e. I am denied freedom of speech and movement. Ironic exaggeration.

30   *clog*, a heavy weight chained to a prisoner's ankle.

31–2   *If ... bite*. Envy was often symbolized by a dog.

35   *use*, profit, advantage.

36   *use it only*, follow or practise it alone as a way of life.

CONRADE: You should hear reason.

DON JOHN: And when I have heard it, what blessing brings it?

CONRADE: If not a present remedy, at least a patient sufferance. 9

DON JOHN: I wonder that thou – being, as thou sayest thou art, born under Saturn – goest about to apply a moral medicine to a mortifying mischief. I cannot hide what I am. I must be sad when I have cause, and smile at no man's jests; eat when I have stomach, and wait for no man's leisure; sleep when I am drowsy, and tend on no man's business; laugh when I am merry, and claw no man in his humour. 17

CONRADE: Yea, but you must not make the full show of this till you may do it without controlment. You have of late stood out against your brother, and he hath ta'en you newly into his grace, where it is impossible you should take true root but by the fair weather that you make yourself. It is needful that you frame the season for your own harvest. 24

DON JOHN: I had rather be a canker in a hedge than a rose in his grace, and it better fits my blood to be disdained of all than to fashion a carriage to rob love from any. In this, though I cannot be said to be a flattering honest man, it must not be denied but I am a plain-dealing villain. I am trusted with a muzzle and enfranchised with a clog; therefore I have decreed not to sing in my cage. If I had my mouth, I would bite; if I had my liberty, I would do my liking. In the meantime, let me be that I am, and seek not to alter me. 34

CONRADE: Can you make no use of your discontent?

DON JOHN: I make all use of it, for I use it only. Who comes here?

39   *yonder*. Any gesture?

41   *intelligence*, news.
42   *model*, a builder's plan for the construction of a house. *mischief*, evil, trouble.
43-4   *What ... unquietness*, what a fool is he who promises to marry a woman.
45   *right hand*, favourite, trusted follower.
46   *exquisite*, choice, select. Contemptuous.

48   *proper squire*, fine gallant. Contemptuous.

52   *forward March-chick*, precocious youngster.

54   *entertained*, taken on, hired.
55   *smoking*, burning fragrant herbs. *musty room*. See I.i location.
56   *sad*, serious.
57   *arras*, tapestry hung on the walls.

62-3   *If ... way*. Antithesis, quibble, repetition, balance.
62   *cross*, (a) make the sign of the cross to bless oneself, (b) thwart, frustrate.
63   *sure*, dependable.

66-7   *Would ... mind*. Why?
67   *prove*, put to the test, try out.

Enter BORACHIO

What news Borachio?

BORACHIO: I came yonder from a great supper. The Prince your brother is royally entertained by Leonato; and I can give you intelligence of an intended marriage.   41

DON JOHN: Will it serve for any model to build mischief on? What is he for a fool that betroths himself to unquietness?

BORACHIO: Marry it is your brother's right hand.

DON JOHN: Who, the most exquisite Claudio?

BORACHIO: Even he.

DON JOHN: A proper squire. And who, and who? Which way looks he?

BORACHIO: Marry on Hero, the daughter and heir of Leonato.   51

DON JOHN: A very forward March-chick. How came you to this?

BORACHIO: Being entertained for a perfumer, as I was smoking a musty room, comes me the Prince and Claudio, hand in hand in sad conference. I whipt me behind the arras, and there heard it agreed upon that the Prince should woo Hero for himself, and having obtained her, give her to Count Claudio.   59

DON JOHN: Come, come, let us thither; this may prove food to my displeasure. That young start-up hath all the glory of my overthrow. If I can cross him any way, I bless myself every way. You are both sure, and will assist me?

CONRADE: To the death my lord.

DON JOHN: Let us to the great supper; their cheer is the greater that I am subdued. Would the cook were o'my mind. Shall we go prove what's to be done?

BORACHIO: We'll wait upon your lordship.   [*Exeunt*

Leonato's house

S.D.   Should the players enter through one door or through different doors? Q, F give no entry for Margaret and Ursula in this scene.

3   *tartly*, sourly.
4   *heart-burned.* Excess of melancholy produced indigestion and a sensation of heart-burning. Beatrice claims that Don John's saturnine melancholy causes that effect in her.

8   *image*, statue.
8–9   *my ... tattling*, i.e. a mother's first-born – and spoilt – son.

15   *if ... will*, if she proved willing. *'a*, he.

17   *shrewd*, sharp.
18   *curst*, cantankerous, bad-tempered.

20–1   *God ... horns*, i.e. God deprives evilly-disposed persons of the means to do harm. Proverbial.

ACT TWO

SCENE ONE

Enter LEONATO, ANTONIO, HERO, BEATRICE, MARGARET, *and* URSULA

LEONATO: Was not Count John here at supper?

ANTONIO: I saw him not.

BEATRICE: How tartly that gentleman looks. I never can see him but I am heart-burned an hour after.

HERO: He is of a very melancholy disposition.

BEATRICE: He were an excellent man that were made just in the midway between him and Benedick. The one is too like an image and says nothing, and the other too like my lady's eldest son, evermore tattling.   9

LEONATO: Then half Signor Benedick's tongue in Count John's mouth, and half Count John's melancholy in Signor Benedick's face –

BEATRICE: With a good leg and a good foot, uncle, and money enough in his purse, such a man would win any woman in the world if 'a could get her good will.

LEONATO: By my troth, niece, thou wilt never get thee a husband if thou be so shrewd of thy tongue.

ANTONIO: In faith she's too curst.

BEATRICE: Too curst is more than curst. I shall lessen God's sending that way; for it is said, 'God sends a curst cow short horns', but to a cow too curst he sends none.   21

LEONATO: So, by being too curst, God will send you no horns.

24   *Just*, exactly, just so. *if ... husband*, i.e. a potential cuckold or
      wearer of horns.

27   *in the woollen*, between rough blankets and not linen sheets.
28   *light on*, chance to find.

31   *more ... youth*, (a) a man, (b) an old man.

34   *in earnest*, in part payment, as a pledge.
35   *bear-ward*, bear-keeper. Bears were kept for the sport of bear-bait-
      ing in which a bear was tied to a stake and savaged by dogs. The
      bear-keeper sometimes kept apes. *lead ... hell*. Proverbially the
      fate of old maids who had not led children into heaven.

39–40 *Get ... maids*. Virgins being pure, did not go to hell but to heaven.
      The Devil in Christian legend received severe rebuffs from such
      virgins as St Pelagia.
40   *maids*, virgins.
41   *Saint ... heavens*. Q and F print a colon after 'Peter'. St Peter,
      the gate-keeper of heaven (*Matt.*, xvi.19). *For the heavens*, by
      heaven. (See *The Merchant of Venice*, II.ii.9.) Some editors change
      the Q, F colon after 'Peter' to a comma, and render the phrase
      'before, or in front of the heavens', or 'in order to reach'.
42   *bachelors*, unmarried men and women. Perhaps an echo of *Rev.*,
      xiv.4. Perhaps too Beatrice should glance at the 'gentlemen's
      rooms' beside the stage.

51–3 *Not ... dust*. See *Gen.*, ii.7, 'The Lord God also did shape man,
      even dust from off the ground'.
51   *metal*, (a) substance, (b) mettle, spirit.
52   *earth*, (a) soil, (b) one of the four elements – earth, air, fire, and
      water – of which man was thought to be made.
53   *valiant dust*. The element earth gave qualities of dullness and
      melancholy to man's constitution. *valiant*, brave, mettlesome.
      Beatrice is mocking.

BEATRICE: Just, if he send me no husband; for the which blessing I am at him upon my knees every morning and evening. Lord, I could not endure a husband with a beard on his face; I had rather lie in the woollen.

LEONATO: You may light on a husband that hath no beard.

BEATRICE: What should I do with him? Dress him in my apparel, and make him my waiting-gentlewoman? He that hath a beard is more than a youth, and he that hath no beard is less than a man; and he that is more than a youth is not for me, and he that is less than a man I am not for him. Therefore I will even take sixpence in earnest of the bear-ward, and lead his apes into hell.   35

LEONATO: Well then, go you into hell?

BEATRICE: No, but to the gate, and there will the devil meet me like an old cuckold with horns on his head, and say 'Get you to heaven, Beatrice, get you to heaven; here's no place for you maids'. So deliver I up my apes, and away to Saint Peter. For the heavens he shows me where the bachelors sit, and there live we as merry as the day is long.

ANTONIO: [To Hero] Well niece, I trust you will be ruled by your father.

BEATRICE: Yes faith, it is my cousin's duty to make curtsy and say, 'Father, as it please you'. But yet for all that, cousin, let him be a handsome fellow, or else make another curtsy and say, 'Father, as it please me'.

LEONATO: Well niece, I hope to see you one day fitted with a husband.   50

BEATRICE: Not till God make men of some other metal than earth. Would it not grieve a woman to be over-mastered with a piece of valiant dust? To make an account

54   *wayward marl*. Marl is a soil containing amounts of lime and formerly used as a top-dressing to fertilize poor land. It was very variable in appearance and composition. *wayward*, perverse, erratic, unmanageable.

55–6   *Adam's . . . kindred*. 'A Table of Kindred and Affinity' printed in the Book of Common Prayer forbad marriage between those who were related within certain degrees of kinship.

55   *brethren*, (a) descendants of Adam, members of the human family, (b) children of the same father.

58   *solicit . . . kind*, i.e. propose marriage to you.

60   *in good time*, (a) soon, at the right time, (b) harmoniously in music, i.e. during the dancing. *important*, pressing, insistent.

61   *measure*, (a) moderation, (b) harmony, (c) dance.

63   *measure*, stately dance. *cinquepace*, lively dance. French 'cinque pas'.

64   *suit*, courtship.

64–5   *full as fantastical*, every bit as wild and odd.

66   *state*, dignity. *ancientry*, old-fashioned stateliness.

66–7   *repentance . . . legs*. Perhaps an emblem figure. In Spenser's *Faerie Queene*, III.xii.24, Repentance is described as 'feeble, sorrowful, and lame'.

67   *cinquepace*. Pronounced 'sink apace'. *faster*. A play on 'apace'.

68   *sink*. A play on 'cinque'.

       Should Beatrice give a mock demonstration of these dances?

69   *apprehend*, grasp, understand. *passing*, exceedingly.

70–1   *I . . . daylight*, i.e. a wedding is clearly coming.

       So far Beatrice's antagonism to marriage is contrasted with Benedick's. Beatrice is teased that she won't get a husband; Benedick that he will get a wife. Is Beatrice's opposition to marriage because – she resents man's domination, men are dull creatures, she has no fear of leading apes to hell, hasty marriage leads to repentance?

S.D.   After Benedick Q has 'and Balthaser, or dumb John'. Dover Wilson modified this to 'Bor(achio), Don John', assuming that the compositor expanded a contraction 'B or' into 'Balthaser or'. Antonio should go out beforehand and return masked.

74   *bout*, turn. Perhaps a formal pairing off and procession round the stage, each couple coming to the front of the stage in turn. *friend*, lover.

of her life to a clod of wayward marl? No, uncle, I'll none.
Adam's sons are my brethren, and truly I hold it a sin to
match in my kindred.

LEONATO: Daughter, remember what I told you. If the
Prince do solicit you in that kind, you know your answer.

BEATRICE: The fault will be in the music cousin, if you be
not wooed in good time. If the Prince be too important,
tell him there is measure in everything, and so dance out
the answer. For hear me Hero: wooing, wedding, and
repenting, is as a Scotch jig, a measure, and a cinquepace;
the first suit is hot and hasty, like a Scotch jig, and full as
fantastical; the wedding, mannerly-modest, as a measure,
full of state and ancientry; and then comes repentance and,
with his bad legs, falls into the cinquepace faster and faster,
till he sink into his grave.   68

LEONATO: Cousin, you apprehend passing shrewdly.

BEATRICE: I have a good eye uncle, I can see a church by
daylight.

LEONATO: The revellers are entering brother, make good
room.

   Enter DON PEDRO, CLAUDIO, BENEDICK, DON
JOHN, BORACHIO *and others, as masquers, with a drummer*

DON PEDRO: Lady, will you walk a bout with your friend?

HERO: So you walk softly, and look sweetly, and say nothing, I am yours for the walk, and especially when I walk
away.

DON PEDRO: With me in your company?

HERO: I may say so when I please.

DON PEDRO: And when please you to say so?   80

81   *favour*, face, looks. *defend*, forbid.

81-2   *the ... case*, i.e. that your face should be like your mask. Masks
       were often grotesque.

83   *visor*, mask. *Philemon's ... Jove*. Ovid (*Metamorphoses*, VIII) told
       how Jupiter and Mercury once wandering on earth were refused
       hospitality by villagers. An old couple, Baucis and Philemon, gave
       them food and shelter in their thatched cottage. An example of
       incongruity which was used again in *As You Like It*, III.iii.7-8.

84   *thatched*. This word was used in Golding's translation of the *Meta-
       morphoses*, which Shakespeare knew. The couplet ll. 83-4 is in the
       same metre as Golding's translation. Is the point that Don Pedro
       was bald?

91   *Amen*, so be it.

95   *Answer, clerk*. Borachio is rebuffed. The clerk was the parish clerk
       who sat by the pulpit and led the responses in church services.

96   *answered*, silenced.

99   *waggling*, shaking with age.

102   *up and down*, all over.

105-7 *Come ... end*. Is Ursula – ironic, flattering, astute, jesting?

106   *mum*, not a word.

HERO : When I like your favour; for God defend the lute should be like the case.

DON PEDRO : My visor is Philemon's roof; within the house is Jove.

HERO : Why then your visor should be thatched.

DON PEDRO : Speak low if you speak of love.

[He draws her aside

BORACHIO : Well, I would you did like me.

MARGARET : So would not I, for your own sake, for I have many ill qualities.

BORACHIO : Which is one?

MARGARET : I say my prayers aloud. 89

BORACHIO : I love you the better; the hearers may cry Amen.

MARGARET : God match me with a good dancer.

BORACHIO : Amen.

MARGARET : And God keep him out of my sight when the dance is done. Answer, clerk.

BORACHIO : No more words, the clerk is answered.

URSULA : I know you well enough, you are Signor Antonio.

ANTONIO : At a word, I am not.

URSULA : I know you by the waggling of your head.

ANTONIO : To tell you true, I counterfeit him. 100

URSULA : You could never do him so ill-well unless you were the very man. Here's his dry hand up and down; you are he, you are he.

ANTONIO : At a word, I am not.

URSULA : Come, come, do you think I do not know you by your excellent wit? Can virtue hide itself? Go to, mum, you are he; graces will appear, and there's an end.

BEATRICE : Will you not tell me who told you so?

BENEDICK : No, you shall pardon me.

BEATRICE : Nor will you not tell me who you are? 110

BENEDICK : Not now.

113   *Hundred Merry Tales*. A popular book of amusing stories each with
        a moral appended, first published in 1526.

120   *jester*, professional clown. *dull*, unamusing, dim-witted.
121   *only his*, his only. *impossible*, unbelievable.
122   *libertines*, unprincipled scoundrels.
123   *villainy*, i.e. slander.
123–4   *for ... them*, i.e. they laugh at his slanders about others and are
        angry at those about themselves.
125   *fleet*, company, throng. *boarded*, accosted.

129–30 *break ... me*, call me a few names. See Falstaff's 'base comparisons'
        against Hal (*I Henry IV*, II.iv.226).
130–1   *which ... melancholy*. See I.i.102–3. Is Benedick – sulky, ignored,
        put out, garrulous, boring?
132   *partridge wing*. Perhaps ironic since Beatrice described Benedick
        as a hearty eater (I.i.45–6).

134–5   *We ... thing*. Proverbial.
134   *leaders*, i.e. in the dance.
        What kind of dance? Sellinger's Round, or a pavane have been
        suggested. The musicians would be placed in a music room above
        stage level. Where are the non-dancers, Leonato, Claudio, Don
        John and Borachio, during the dance? How do the players with-
        draw?
138–9   *Sure ... it*. Does Don John believe this, or is it the sudden birth
        of a device to cause trouble?

BEATRICE: That I was disdainful, and that I had my good
    wit out of the 'Hundred Merry Tales' – well, this was
    Signor Benedick that said so.

BENEDICK: What's he?

BEATRICE: I am sure you know him well enough.

BENEDICK: Not I, believe me.

BEATRICE: Did he never make you laugh?

BENEDICK: I pray you what is he?   119

BEATRICE: Why, he is the Prince's jester, a very dull fool;
    only his gift is in devising impossible slanders. None but
    libertines delight in him, and the commendation is not
    in his wit, but in his villainy; for he both pleases men
    and angers them, and then they laugh at him and beat
    him. I am sure he is in the fleet; I would he had boarded
    me.

BENEDICK: When I know the gentleman, I'll tell him what
    you say.   128

BEATRICE: Do, do; he'll but break a comparison or two
    on me, which peradventure not marked or not laughed
    at, strikes him into melancholy; and then there's a
    partridge wing saved, for the fool will eat no supper that
    night.

                                        [*Music for the dance*

We must follow the leaders.

BENEDICK: In every good thing.

BEATRICE: Nay, if they lead to any ill, I will leave them at
    the next turning.

                        [*Dance. Then exeunt all except Don John,*
                                        Borachio, and Claudio

DON JOHN: Sure my brother is amorous on Hero, and hath
    withdrawn her father to break with him about it. The
    ladies follow her, and but one visor remains.   140

BORACHIO: And that is Claudio; I know him by his
    bearing.

151–2   *I ... tonight.* Is this something misheard or a deliberate lie?

153   *banquet.* Light refreshment consisting mainly of sweets, fruit, and wine, after the dance.

154–5   *Thus ... Claudio.* Shakespeare makes sure the audience is not confused.

157–8   *Friendship ... love.* A version of the proverb, 'When love puts in, friendship is gone'.

158   *office*, business.

159   *use*, let them use.

162   *faith*, loyalty. *blood*, passion, lust.

163   *This ... proof*, such an event is frequently experienced.
        Why is Claudio given eleven lines of verse in the middle of prose – to mark the love theme, to stress his own gullibility or uncertainty, to emphasize the importance of the soliloquy?
        Is Claudio – lacking confidence, uncertain, faint-hearted, gullible, adolescent, credulous?

169   *willow.* The emblem of forsaken or unrequited love.

170   *County*, count.

DON JOHN: Are not you Signor Benedick?

CLAUDIO: You know me well; I am he.

DON JOHN: Signor, you are very near my brother in his love. He is enamoured on Hero; I pray you dissuade him from her; she is no equal for his birth. You may do the part of an honest man in it.

CLAUDIO: How know you he loves her?

DON JOHN: I heard him swear his affection.   150

BORACHIO: So I did too, and he swore he would marry her tonight.

DON JOHN: Come, let us to the banquet.

> [*Exeunt Don John and Borachio*

CLAUDIO: Thus answer I in name of Benedick,
But hear these ill news with the ears of Claudio.
'Tis certain so; the Prince woos for himself.
Friendship is constant in all other things
Save in the office and affairs of love.
Therefore all hearts in love use their own tongues.
Let every eye negotiate for itself,   160
And trust no agent; for beauty is a witch
Against whose charms faith melteth into blood.
This is an accident of hourly proof,
Which I mistrusted not. Farewell therefore Hero.

Enter BENEDICK

BENEDICK: Count Claudio?

CLAUDIO: Yea, the same.

BENEDICK: Come, will you go with me?

CLAUDIO: Whither?   168

BENEDICK: Even to the next willow, about your own business, County. What fashion will you wear the garland

171–2   *About ... scarf.* Usually taken to mean that Claudio should demand satisfaction from Don Pedro either by monetary compensation or by fighting a duel.

171   *usurer's chain.* Wealthy men such as money-lenders often wore a lengthy gold chain round their necks.

172   *lieutenant's scarf.* The sash worn diagonally from shoulder to hip by an officer.

174   *I ... her.* A wish sometimes expressed by the seller at the conclusion of a bargain. See *Antony and Cleopatra*, V.ii.257. Is this spoken – gravely, bitterly, graciously, sulkily, carelessly?

175   *drover,* cattle-dealer.

179–80   *Now ... post,* now you are hitting out wildly at the wrong man. See Appendix II.

181   *If ... be,* if you will not leave me.

187   *though.* Dover Wilson has 'the', Johnson's emendation, arguing a mistake of 'tho' for 'the'. *bitter ... Beatrice.* Is there a quibble on 'bitter', 'Beatrice'. Beatrice was a two-syllable word pronounced Beetris (see III.i.21, 24, 29). Is her tongue bitter?

187–8   *puts ... person,* imagines that everyone thinks as she does.

188   *gives me out,* makes me out to be, represents me.

192   *Troth,* in truth.

192–3   *Lady Fame,* i.e. spreader of rumours.

193–4   *melancholy ... warren.* A warren was a large piece of land where rabbits and hares were encouraged to breed. The lodge was the warrener's (game-keeper's) house isolated in the midst of the warren and sometimes fortified to protect the warrener from attacks by poachers. One such remains near Thetford, Norfolk.

194–5   *I ... lady.* Benedick, who does not know of the arrangement, accuses the Duke of stealing Hero's love.

197–8   *bind ... rod,* i.e. use a bundle of twigs to make a birch-rod.

200   *flat,* downright.

of? About your neck, like an usurer's chain? Or under your arm, like a lieutenant's scarf? You must wear it one way, for the Prince hath got your Hero.

CLAUDIO: I wish him joy of her.

BENEDICK: Why, that's spoken like an honest drover; so they sell bullocks. But did you think the Prince would have served you thus?

CLAUDIO: I pray you leave me.   178

BENEDICK: Ho! Now you strike like the blind man; 'twas the boy that stole your meat, and you'll beat the post.

CLAUDIO: If it will not be, I'll leave you.   [*Exit*

BENEDICK: Alas poor hurt fowl, now will he creep into sedges. But that my Lady Beatrice should know me, and not know me. The Prince's fool! Ha, it may be I go under that title because I am merry. Yea but so I am apt to do myself wrong. I am not so reputed; it is the base, though bitter, disposition of Beatrice that puts the world into her person, and so gives me out. Well, I'll be revenged as I may.   189

Enter DON PEDRO, LEONATO, *and* HERO

DON PEDRO: Now signor, where's the Count? Did you see him?

BENEDICK: Troth my lord, I have played the part of Lady Fame. I found him here as melancholy as a lodge in a warren. I told him, and I think I told him true, that your grace had got the good will of this young lady; and I offered him my company to a willow-tree, either to make him a garland, as being forsaken, or to bind him up a rod, as being worthy to be whipped.

DON PEDRO: To be whipped? What's his fault?   199

BENEDICK: The flat transgression of a schoolboy, who, being overjoyed with finding a bird's nest, shows it his companion, and he steals it.

209   *them*, young birds.

211   *answer*, confirms.

213   *The ... you.* Is this correct?

216   *misused*, abused, slandered.
217   *block,?* chopping-block.

221   *a great thaw*, i.e. dull foggy and dispiriting weather during a thaw.
222   *impossible conveyance*, incredible flow of words.
222–3   *man ... mark*, marker at an archery butt.
224   *poniards*, daggers.
225   *terminations*, terms, expressions, epithets. There is something of
        a quibble here between 'breath', (a) air expelled, (b) speech, and
        'terminations'.
226   *infect ... star*, bring disease to the uttermost bounds of space. Stars
        were symbols of purity and incorruptibility.
227–8   *all ... him*, all to which he was heir.
228–30 *She ... too.* In classical legend Hercules, to make amends for the
        crime of murder, was sold as a slave to Queen Omphale of Lydia.
        She dressed him in female clothes and employed him in women's
        tasks, while she wore his lion skin and bore his club. See II.i.29–
        30.

DON PEDRO : Wilt thou make a trust a transgression? The transgression is in the stealer.

BENEDICK : Yet it had not been amiss the rod had been made, and the garland too; for the garland he might have worn himself, and the rod he might have bestowed on you, who, as I take it, have stolen his bird's nest.

DON PEDRO : I will but teach them to sing, and restore them to the owner.   210

BENEDICK : If their singing answer your saying, by my faith you say honestly.

DON PEDRO : The Lady Beatrice hath a quarrel to you. The gentleman that danced with her told her she is much wronged by you.   215

BENEDICK : O she misused me past the endurance of a block. An oak but with one green leaf on it would have answered her; my very visor began to assume life and scold with her. She told me, not thinking I had been myself, that I was the Prince's jester, that I was duller than a great thaw; huddling jest upon jest with such impossible conveyance upon me that I stood like a man at a mark, with a whole army shooting at me. She speaks poniards, and every word stabs. If her breath were as terrible as her terminations, there were no living near her; she would infect to the north star. I would not marry her, though she were endowed with all that Adam had left him before he transgressed. She would have made Hercules have turned spit, yea, and have cleft his club to make the fire too. Come, talk not of her. You shall find her the

231   *infernal Ate*, the classical goddess of discord from the underworld.
       Ate was the goddess of mischief cast down from Olympus by
       Jupiter. She stirred up men to discord through folly and moral
       blindness. Shakespeare seems to link her with Discordia, who
       lived with the Furies in the underworld, and who was dressed
       in a torn robe, and who wore a dagger. See *Julius Caesar*, III.i.271.

232   *scholar ... her*. Hellish spirits could be exorcized only by scholars
       who could speak the Latin service of exorcism. *conjure*, cast out
       evil spirits from her.

233   *as ... sanctuary*, i.e. hell by comparison is as peaceful as a place
       of holy refuge.

235   *all ... pertubation*, i.e. the attributes of hell.

239   *Antipodes*. Places on the opposite side of the globe whose inhabi-
       tants' feet are opposed to ours.

240   *tooth-picker*. Toothpicks made of gold and ornamented with
       jewels were often imported from the orient.

241   *Prester John*, Priest John. The name given in the Middle Ages to
       an alleged Christian priest and king, originally supposed to reign
       in China, but later identified with the king of Ethiopia.

242   *great Cham's*, the Emperor of China's.

243   *Pigmies*, races of small men supposed according to ancient history
       and tradition to live in various parts of India and Africa.

244   *harpy*, a fabulous, voracious creature, having a woman's face and
       body with a bird's wings and claws. It sometimes acted as a
       minister of divine vengeance. See *The Tempest*, III.iii.52 S.D.

246   *dish*, (a) kind of food, (b) used disparagingly of a woman: Cleopa-
       tra was Antony's 'Egyptian dish'. See *Antony and Cleopatra*,
       II.vi.121; V.ii.270–1; *Pericles*, IV.vi.160. 'Lady Tongue' combines
       both meanings. Is Benedick over-protesting with his hyperboles
       and extravaganzas?

248–53 *you ... it*. What significance has this?

254   *put him down*, silenced him.

260   *sad*, serious, gloomy.

infernal Ate in good apparel. I would to God some scholar would conjure her; for certainly, while she is here, a man may live as quiet in hell as in a sanctuary, and people sin upon purpose, because they would go thither; so indeed all disquiet, horror, and perturbation follows her.

Enter CLAUDIO *and* BEATRICE

DON PEDRO: Look, here she comes.   236

BENEDICK: Will your grace command me any service to the world's end? I will go on the slightest errand now to the Antipodes that you can devise to send me on. I will fetch you a tooth-picker now from the furthest inch of Asia; bring you the length of Prester John's foot; fetch you a hair off the great Cham's beard; do you an embassage to the Pigmies, rather than hold three words' conference with this harpy. You have no employment for me?

DON PEDRO: None, but to desire your good company.

BENEDICK: O God sir, here's a dish I love not; I cannot endure my Lady Tongue.   [*Exit*

DON PEDRO: Come lady, come; you have lost the heart of Signor Benedick.   249

BEATRICE: Indeed my lord, he lent it me awhile, and I gave him use for it, a double heart for his single one. Marry, once before he won it of me with false dice, therefore your grace may well say I have lost it.

DON PEDRO: You have put him down lady, you have put him down.

BEATRICE: So I would not he should do me, my lord, lest I should prove the mother of fools. I have brought Count Claudio, whom you sent me to seek.

DON PEDRO: Why, how now Count. Wherefore are you sad?   260

CLAUDIO: Not sad, my lord.

DON PEDRO: How then? Sick?

265   *civil*, (a) sober, decent, (b) Seville.
266   *jealous complexion*, i.e. yellow and bitter. *complexion*, (a) temperament, (b) colour of skin.
267   *blazon*, description (heraldic term).
268   *conceit*, idea, notion.

270   *broke with*, spoken on the matter with. *will*, willingness.

273-4   *all grace say*. F 'may God say'.
275-7   *Speak ... much*. Some have condemned Claudio for his silence. But elsewhere in Shakespeare the lover 'being wholly employed in the contemplation ... of the thing beloved' is in ecstasy and bereft of words (Bamborough, *The Little World of Man*, p. 126). Proverbially 'whom we love best to them we can say least'.
276   *Silence ... joy*. Paradox.
278-9   *dote upon*, cherish.

283   *fool*, dear, innocent.
284   *windy side*, to the windward as deer keeps away from the scent of trouble, or a sailing ship so keeps the advantage of manœuvre against an enemy.
287   *Good ... alliance*, good heavens, how marriages are in favour. Some see this as a retort to Claudio's claim to cousinship.
287-8   *goes ... world*, everyone marries.
288   *sunburnt*, i.e. out of fashion, despised. A fair, white complexion was favoured by Elizabethan ladies. *sit ... corner*, be neglected, be alone.
289   *Heigh-ho ... husband*. The title of a ballad, 'Heigh-ho for a husband, or the willing maid's wants known'. *Heigh-ho*, sigh.
291   *getting*, begetting.

CLAUDIO: Neither, my lord.

BEATRICE: The Count is neither sad, nor sick, nor merry, nor well; but civil count, civil as an orange, and something of that jealous complexion.

DON PEDRO: I'faith lady, I think your blazon to be true, though I'll be sworn, if he be so, his conceit is false. Here Claudio, I have wooed in thy name, and fair Hero is won. I have broke with her father, and his will obtained; name the day of marriage, and God give thee joy. 271

LEONATO: Count, take of me my daughter, and with her my fortunes. His grace hath made the match, and all grace say Amen to it.

BEATRICE: Speak Count, 'tis your cue.

CLAUDIO: Silence is the perfectest herald of joy; I were but little happy, if I could say how much. Lady, as you are mine, I am yours; I give away myself for you and dote upon the exchange.

BEATRICE: Speak cousin, or, if you cannot, stop his mouth with a kiss, and let not him speak neither. 281

DON PEDRO: In faith lady, you have a merry heart.

BEATRICE: Yea my lord, I thank it, poor fool, it keeps on the windy side of care. My cousin tells him in his ear that he is in her heart.

CLAUDIO: And so she doth, cousin.

BEATRICE: Good Lord, for alliance! Thus goes every one to the world but I, and I am sunburnt. I may sit in a corner and cry 'Heigh-ho for a husband'.

DON PEDRO: Lady Beatrice, I will get you one. 290

BEATRICE: I would rather have one of your father's getting. Hath your grace ne'er a brother like you? Your father got excellent husbands, if a maid could come by them.

DON PEDRO: Will you have me, lady?

BEATRICE: No my lord, unless I might have another for

297–8   *I ... matter*. Beatrice apologizes for treating the Duke's offer lightly.

298   *matter*, sense.

303   *star ... born*. By its influence gave her a merry disposition.

307   *cry you mercy*, beg your pardon. Any movement?

310   *melancholy element*, (a) black bile, (b) gloom, despondency.

312   *ever* Q. Some emend to 'even'.

317   *suit*, wooing.

323–4   *Time ... rites*. Time was sometimes represented by Renaissance artists as an old man with crutches.

326   *a just seven-night*, exactly a week.
327   *answer my mind*, satisfy my intentions.
328–9   *breathing*, pause, delay.

working-days; your grace is too costly to wear every day. But I beseech your grace pardon me, I was born to speak all mirth and no matter.

DON PEDRO: Your silence most offends me, and to be merry best becomes you; for out o'question, you were born in a merry hour. 301

BEATRICE: No sure my lord, my mother cried; but then there was a star danced, and under that was I born. Cousins, God give you joy.

LEONATO: Niece, will you look to those things I told you of?

BEATRICE: I cry you mercy uncle. [*To Don Pedro*] By your grace's pardon. [*Exit*

DON PEDRO: By my troth a pleasant-spirited lady. 309

LEONATO: There's little of the melancholy element in her my lord. She is never sad but when she sleeps, and not ever sad then; for I have heard my daughter say, she hath often dreamt of unhappiness and waked herself with laughing.

DON PEDRO: She cannot endure to hear tell of a husband.

LEONATO: O by no means; she mocks all her wooers out of suit.

DON PEDRO: She were an excellent wife for Benedick.

LEONATO: O Lord, my lord, if they were but a week married, they would talk themselves mad. 320

DON PEDRO: County Claudio, when mean you to go to church?

CLAUDIO: Tomorrow my lord. Time goes on crutches till love have all his rites.

LEONATO: Not till Monday, my dear son, which is hence a just seven-night; and a time too brief too, to have all things answer my mind. 327

DON PEDRO: Come, you shake the head at so long a breathing, but I warrant thee Claudio, the time shall not go dully

330–1   *one ... labours*, i.e. an enormous task. In classical story Hercules, son of Jupiter and Alcmena, in a fit of madness slew his children. As a punishment twelve labours were imposed on him.

337   *nights' watchings*, nights without sleep.

340   *modest office*, part in keeping with my modesty.
344   *strain*, family. *approved*, well tried. *honesty*, honour.
347   *practise on*, work on.
348   *queasy stomach*, fastidious taste.
350   *only*, supreme.
351   *drift*, what's in my mind.
        This scene prepares for two actions: the wedding of Hero and Claudio, and the manœuvring into love of Benedick and Beatrice. Don John's partly successful intrigue makes manifest aspects of character and attitudes of mind that influence subsequent events: Claudio's vulnerability, credulity, and immaturity; Don Pedro's integrity (see IV.i.150). Don Pedro, arrogantly over-confident, challenges Cupid (ll. 349–50), as Benedick had done previously (I.i.35ff, 224–5, 241); both invite downfall. Benedick and Beatrice protest too much, a barrage of witticisms conceals their true selves; but there are intimations that marriage is in the minds of both, and Beatrice mentions a previous exchange of hearts.

Leonato's house

1–2   *It ... Leonato*. Device of continued conversation. Is Don John – vexed, furious, reflective, insistent, disgusted, frustrated?
1   *shall*, is to.
3   *cross*, prevent.
4   *cross*, obstacle.
5   *medicinable*, medicinal.

by us. I will in the interim undertake one of Hercules'
labours, which is to bring Signor Benedick and the Lady
Beatrice into a mountain of affection th'one with th'other.
I would fain have it a match; and I doubt not but to
fashion it if you three will but minister such assistance as I
shall give you direction.

LEONATO: My lord, I am for you, though it cost me ten
nights' watchings.

CLAUDIO: And I my lord.

DON PEDRO: And you too, gentle Hero?

HERO: I will do any modest office, my lord, to help my
cousin to a good husband.   341

DON PEDRO: And Benedick is not the unhopefullest husband that I know. Thus far can I praise him: he is of a
noble strain, of approved valour, and confirmed honesty.
I will teach you how to humour your cousin, that she shall
fall in love with Benedick; and I, with your two helps,
will so practise on Benedick that, in despite of his quick
wit and his queasy stomach, he shall fall in love with
Beatrice. If we can do this, Cupid is no longer an archer;
his glory shall be ours, for we are the only love-gods. Go
in with me, and I will tell you my drift.   [*Exeunt*

SCENE TWO

Enter DON JOHN *and* BORACHIO

DON JOHN: It is so; the Count Claudio shall marry the
daughter of Leonato.

BORACHIO: Yea my lord, but I can cross it.

DON JOHN: Any bar, any cross, any impediment will be
medicinable to me. I am sick in displeasure to him, and

6–7 *whatsoever ... mine*, whatever cuts across his desires is in keeping with mine.
8 *covertly*, secretly.

16 *appoint*, arrange with.
17 *life ... death*. Paradox. *life*, power.

19 *temper*, compound, concoct.
20 *spare not*, do not fail.

22 *estimation*, worth.
23 *contaminated stale*, polluted prostitute.

25 *misuse*, abuse, deceive. *vex*, agonize.
26 *undo*, ruin.

28 *despite*, work ill upon.

30 *meet hour*, convenient time.

32 *intend*, pretend. *zeal*, earnestness, ardent care.

35 *cozened*, cheated, deceived. *semblance*, outward appearance.
36 *maid*, virgin.
37 *trial*, question, verification. *instances*, examples.
37–8 *shall ... likelihood*, shall be nothing less.
39–40 *hear ... Claudio*. Much discussed. It seems best to assume that Borachio and Margaret play a game of 'let's pretend' with Margaret putting on Hero's dress (V.i.224). In this way Margaret is innocent of complicity in the plot as Borachio testifies (V.i.285–8). However, this is hardly clear to the audience.

whatsoever comes athwart his affection ranges evenly with
mine. How canst thou cross this marriage?

BORACHIO: Not honestly my lord, but so covertly that no
dishonesty shall appear in me.

DON JOHN: Show me briefly how.   10

BORACHIO: I think I told your lordship a year since, how
much I am in the favour of Margaret, the waiting-
gentlewoman to Hero.

DON JOHN: I remember.

BORACHIO: I can, at any unseasonable instant of the night,
appoint her to look out at her lady's chamber-window.

DON JOHN: What life is in that, to be the death of this
marriage?   18

BORACHIO: The poison of that lies in you to temper. Go
you to the Prince your brother; spare not to tell him
that he hath wronged his honour in marrying the re-
nowned Claudio – whose estimation do you mightily hold
up – to a contaminated stale, such a one as Hero.

DON JOHN: What proof shall I make of that?

BORACHIO: Proof enough to misuse the Prince, to vex
Claudio, to undo Hero, and kill Leonato. Look you for
any other issue?

DON JOHN: Only to despite them I will endeavour anything.   29

BORACHIO: Go then, find me a meet hour to draw Don
Pedro and the Count Claudio alone. Tell them that you
know that Hero loves me; intend a kind of zeal both to
the Prince and Claudio as – in love of your brother's
honour, who hath made this match, and his friend's reputation, who is thus like to be cozened with the semblance of
a maid – that you have discovered thus. They will scarcely
believe this without trial. Offer them instances, which shall
bear no less likelihood than to see me at her chamber
window, hear me call Margaret Hero, hear Margaret term

44 *jealousy ... assurance*, jealous suspicion shall be taken as confirmation. *preparation*, i.e. for the wedding.

49 *constant*, persevering, steadfast.

51 *presently*, immediately.

Leonato's orchard

Some stage properties are required: trees, shrubs, benches, seats. How should the arbour be constructed and sited so that its occupant can be seen and heard by the audience?

5 *I ... already*, done as soon as said.
   What is the point of this exchange with the Boy – to indicate location in view of the eavesdropping, to suggest that Benedick wishes to be alone? There are no stage directions for the Boy. Suggest some.

10 *argument*, subject.

me Claudio; and bring them to see this the very night before the intended wedding – for in the meantime I will so fashion the matter that Hero shall be absent – and there shall appear such seeming truth of Hero's disloyalty that jealousy shall be called assurance, and all the preparation overthrown.

DON JOHN: Grow this to what adverse issue it can, I will put it in practice. Be cunning in the working this, and thy fee is a thousand ducats.

BORACHIO: Be you constant in the accusation, and my cunning shall not shame me.   50

DON JOHN: I will presently go learn their day of marriage.

[*Exeunt*

SCENE THREE

Enter BENEDICK *alone*

BENEDICK: Boy!

Enter BOY

BOY: Signor.

BENEDICK: In my chamber-window lies a book, bring it hither to me in the orchard.

BOY: I am here already sir.   5

BENEDICK: I know that, but I would have thee hence and here again.[*Exit Boy*] I do much wonder that one man, seeing how much another man is a fool when he dedicates his behaviours to love, will, after he hath laughed at such shallow follies in others, become the argument of his own scorn by falling in love; and such a man is Claudio. I have

12   *with him*, in his opinion.

12–13   *drum ... fife*, i.e. martial music.

13   *fife*, a small, shrill, flute-like instrument.

13–14   *tabor ... pipe*. Both were associated with social gatherings and entertainments.

14   *pipe*, small recorder.

16   *carving*, shaping.

18   *turned orthography*, uses ornate expressions of speech.

19   *fantastical banquet*, feast of flights of fancy.

24, 25 *fair, wise, virtuous*. See ll. 216–18. *well*, i.e. uninfected with love.

25–6   *all ... grace*. Antimetabole – neatly condensing the thought.

28   *cheapen*, offer for.

29   *noble*, (a) coin, three to a £, (b) high born. *angel*, (a) coin, two to a £, (b) heavenly messenger.

30   *discourse*, conversation.

30–1   *her ... God*, i.e. natural, not dyed.
        Is Benedick – misogynistic, hesitant, irresolute, astonished, weakening, fearful, fastidious, uneasy?

S.D.   Q 'Enter prince, Leonato, Claudio, Musicke'.
        F 'Enter Prince, Leonato, Claudio, and Jacke Wilson'.
        Q alone has a further entry at l.38, 'Enter Balthasar with musicke'. Jack Wilson, the singer who took Balthasar's part, is not otherwise known. Attempts to identify him with Dr John Wilson, professor of music at Oxford in 1656, are not convincing.

34–5   *How ... harmony*. Is this a hint to the audience to keep quiet?

38   *fit ... pennyworth*, see to it that the lurking eavesdropper gets his money's worth. *hid-fox*. Q 'kid-fox'. Perhaps a reference to a game as in *Hamlet*, IV.ii.28, 'Hide fox, and all after'.

40   *tax not*, do not compel. It has been suggested that Balthasar is not a professional singer but an amateur, hesitant over his ability as a singer, like Amiens in *As You Like It*.

41   *slander*, ruin.

42   *the witness still*, always the proof.

known when there was no music with him but the drum
and the fife, and now had he rather hear the tabor and the
pipe. I have known when he would have walked ten mile
afoot to see a good armour, and now will he lie ten nights
awake carving the fashion of a new doublet. He was wont
to speak plain and to the purpose, like an honest man and
a soldier, and now is he turned orthography; his words are
a very fantastical banquet, just so many strange dishes. May
I be so converted and see with these eyes? I cannot tell – I
think not. I will not be sworn but love may transform
me to an oyster; but I'll take my oath on it, till he have
made an oyster of me, he shall never make me such a fool.
One woman is fair, yet I am well; another is wise, yet I
am well; another virtuous, yet I am well. But till all graces
be in one woman, one woman shall not come in my grace.
Rich she shall be, that's certain; wise, or I'll none; virtuous,
or I'll never cheapen her; fair, or I'll never look on her;
mild, or come not near me; noble, or not I for an angel;
of good discourse, an excellent musician, and her hair shall
be of what colour it please God. Ha, the Prince and
Monsieur Love! I will hide me in the arbour.   32

Enter DON PEDRO, LEONATO, CLAUDIO, *and* BALTHASAR

DON PEDRO: Come, shall we hear this music?
CLAUDIO: Yea my good lord. How still the evening is,
    As hushed on purpose to grace harmony.
DON PEDRO: See you where Benedick hath hid himself?
CLAUDIO: O very well my lord; the music ended,
    We'll fit the hid-fox with a pennyworth.
DON PEDRO: Come Balthasar, we'll hear that song again.
BALTHASAR: O good my lord, tax not so bad a voice
    To slander music any more than once.   41
DON PEDRO: It is the witness still of excellency

43   *put ... on*, view unfavourably, or, pretend not to know.
44   *woo*, beg you.

47   *not worthy*, (a) unworthy, (b) ? quibble on 'noteworthy'.

50   *notes*, (a) musical notes, (b) brief forms – a glance at 'longer argu-
       ment'.
51   *noting*, (a) paying attention to, (b) recording in a musical score.
52   *crotchets*, (a) whims, quirks, (b) musical notes.
53   *Note ... nothing*, attend to the notes and to nothing else. *nothing*,
       (a) nothing, (b) noting.
       The twenty-one lines of blank verse that contain Balthasar's pro-
       testations (much ado about noting) and Don Pedro's insistence
       that he shall sing are a preparation for the deceiving of Benedick.
       The harmony of the verse, the link indicated between wooing
       and music, the mirror-like reflection of Benedick's attitudes, i.e.
       lack of harmony and love in Balthasar's protests, are pointed
       directly at Benedick.
54   *Now divine air*. The preliminary notes perhaps played by Balthasar
       on a lute.
54–6 *Now ... bodies*. The power of music to entrance men is mentioned
       frequently by Shakespeare: *Twelfth Night*, *The Merchant of Venice*,
       and *The Tempest*. Some believed that the soul was itself a form
       of harmony.
55   *sheep's guts*. Used for the strings of musical instruments. *hale*, pull.
       Is Benedick ironic?
56   *a ... money*, i.e. I prefer a trumpet (or hunting horn). Perhaps an
       ironic reference to the cuckold's horn.
S.D.   *The Song*. A contemporary setting by T. Ford is printed arranged
       as a solo in P. Warlock, *Four English Songs of the Early Seventeenth
       Century* (F. W. Sternfeld, *Music in Shakespearean Tragedy*). Should
       Don Pedro and his companions sit aside to listen?
60   *One ... shore*. Perhaps an allusion to Fortune, depicted as a woman
       on a rolling terrestrial globe.

To put a strange face on his own perfection.
I pray thee sing, and let me woo no more.

BALTHASAR: Because you talk of wooing, I will sing,
Since many a wooer doth commence his suit
To her he thinks not worthy, yet he woos,
Yet will he swear he loves.

DON PEDRO: Nay pray thee come,
Or if thou wilt hold longer argument,
Do it in notes.

BALTHASAR: Note this before my notes;   50
There's not a note of mine that's worth the noting.

DON PEDRO: Why these are very crotchets that he speaks;
Note notes forsooth, and nothing.

                                            [*Music*

BENEDICK: Now divine air. Now is his soul ravished. Is
it not strange that sheep's guts should hale souls out of
men's bodies? Well, a horn for my money when all's
done.

The Song

BALTHASAR:
          Sigh no more, ladies, sigh no more,
            Men were deceivers ever,
          One foot in sea and one on shore,   60
            To one thing constant never.
          Then sigh not so, but let them go,
            And be you blithe and bonny,
          Converting all your sounds of woe
            Into Hey nonny, nonny.

66   *ditties*, songs. *moe*, more.
67   *dumps*, (a) sorrows, (b) sad songs.
       The theme of the song could not only refer to Beatrice who talked
       of sighing for a husband and had lost Benedick's heart by his cheat-
       ing, but also prepare for the love-stricken Beatrice they are about
       to describe.

77   *for a shift*, as a makeshift, or perhaps, for our special purpose.
78   *An*, if.
79–81 *I ... it*. Ironically it does forebode mischief for Benedick.
80   *bode*, foretell. *lief*, gladly.
81   *night-raven*, raven, or owl, whose call was thought to foretell death
       or illness.
82   *Yea marry*. Don Pedro, Claudio, and Leonato have been talking
       aside during Benedick's speech.
82–4 *I ... window*. Nothing more is heard of this.

89   *stalk ... sits*, nearer, nearer, the bird has settled. *stalk*. A fowler
       used to approach a sitting bird under cover of a horse or cow,
       or a canvas imitation of one.
91   *wonderful*, extraordinary.
92   *dote so*, be so infatuated with.

94–5 *Sits ... corner*, is the wind blowing from that direction, is that the
       way matters are?

97   *enraged*, passionate, intense, fierce.
98   *it ... thought*, it is beyond the bounds of doubt.

Sing no more ditties, sing no moe,
  Of dumps so dull and heavy,
The fraud of men was ever so,
  Since summer first was leavy.
Then sigh not so, but let them go,   70
  And be you blithe and bonny,
Converting all your sounds of woe
  Into Hey nonny, nonny.

DON PEDRO: By my troth a good song.

BALTHASAR: And an ill singer my lord.

DON PEDRO: Ha, no, no faith, thou sing'st well enough for a shift.

BENEDICK: An he had been a dog that should have howled thus, they would have hanged him; and I pray God his bad voice bode no mischief. I had as lief have heard the night-raven, come what plague could have come after it.

DON PEDRO: Yea marry, dost thou hear, Balthasar? I pray thee, get us some excellent music; for tomorrow night we would have it at the Lady Hero's chamber-window.

BALTHASAR: The best I can my lord.   85

DON PEDRO: Do so; farewell. [*Exit Balthasar*] Come hither Leonato. What was it you told me of today, that your niece Beatrice was in love with Signor Benedick?

CLAUDIO: [*Aside*] O ay, stalk on, stalk on, the fowl sits. – I did never think that lady would have loved any man. 90

LEONATO: No nor I neither; but most wonderful that she should dote so on Signor Benedick, whom she hath in all outward behaviours seemed ever to abhor.

BENEDICK: [*Aside*] Is't possible? Sits the wind in that corner?

LEONATO: By my troth my lord, I cannot tell what to think of it; but that she loves him with an enraged affection – it is past the infinite of thought.

102   *life of,* living.
103   *discovers,* reveals.

107–8   *you ... how.* Does Leonato's inspiration fail, or is this a device to rouse Benedick's curiosity?

115   *gull,* trick.
116   *white-bearded fellow.* Leonato's age is noted elsewhere (I.i.100, V.i.56).

118–9   *ta'en th'infection,* swallowed the bait.
119   *hold it up,* keep it up.

128   *write to him.* See V.iv.88–9.
129   *smock,* chemise, vest. Elizabethan women slept either naked or in their underclothes.

132   *pretty,* clever.

DON PEDRO: May be she doth but counterfeit.

CLAUDIO: Faith, like enough. 100

LEONATO: O God, counterfeit? There was never counterfeit of passion came so near the life of passion as she discovers it.

DON PEDRO: Why what effects of passion shows she?

CLAUDIO: [*To Don Pedro and Leonato*] Bait the hook well, this fish will bite.

LEONATO: What effects, my lord? She will sit you – you heard my daughter tell you how.

CLAUDIO: She did indeed. 109

DON PEDRO: How, how I pray you? You amaze me. I would have thought her spirit had been invincible against all assaults of affection.

LEONATO: I would have sworn it had, my lord, especially against Benedick.

BENEDICK: [*Aside*] I should think this a gull, but that the white-bearded fellow speaks it; knavery cannot sure hide himself in such reverence.

CLAUDIO: [*To Don Pedro and Leonato*] He hath ta'en th' infection; hold it up. 119

DON PEDRO: Hath she made her affection known to Benedick?

LEONATO: No, and swears she never will – that's her torment.

CLAUDIO: 'Tis true indeed, so your daughter says. 'Shall I,' says she, 'that have so oft encountered him with scorn, write to him that I love him?'

LEONATO: This says she now when she is beginning to write to him; for she'll be up twenty times a night, and there will she sit in her smock till she have writ a sheet of paper – my daughter tells us all. 130

CLAUDIO: Now you talk of a sheet of paper, I remember a pretty jest your daughter told us of.

134   *sheet*, (a) writing paper, (b) bed linen.
135   *That*, that's it.
136   *halfpence*, fragments. The halfpenny was a small silver coin.
137   *railed at*, scolded.
138   *flout*, scorn.

144   *my ... so*. Leonato suddenly remembers that he could not have seen it.
145   *ecstasy*, frenzy.
146   *desperate outrage*, violent injury, despairing violence.

152   *alms*, charitable deed.

157   *blood*, passion.

161   *dotage*, infatuation.
162   *daffed ... respects*, put aside all differences of rank.
163   *'a*, he.

LEONATO: O, when she had writ it and was reading it over, she found Benedick and Beatrice between the sheet?

CLAUDIO: That.

LEONATO: O, she tore the letter into a thousand halfpence; railed at herself that she should be so immodest to write to one that she knew would flout her. 'I measure him,' says she, 'by my own spirit; for I should flout him if he writ to me; yea though I love him, I should.'   140

CLAUDIO: Then down upon her knees she falls, weeps, sobs, beats her heart, tears her hair, prays, curses – 'O sweet Benedick! God give me patience.'

LEONATO: She doth indeed – my daughter says so. And the ecstasy hath so much overborne her that my daughter is sometime afeard she will do a desperate outrage to herself. It is very true.

DON PEDRO: It were good that Benedick knew of it by some other, if she will not discover it.   149

CLAUDIO: To what end? He would make but a sport of it and torment the poor lady worse.

DON PEDRO: An he should, it were an alms to hang him. She's an excellent sweet lady, and, out of all suspicion, she is virtuous.

CLAUDIO: And she is exceeding wise.

DON PEDRO: In every thing but in loving Benedick.

LEONATO: O my lord, wisdom and blood combating in so tender a body, we have ten proofs to one that blood hath the victory. I am sorry for her, as I have just cause, being her uncle and her guardian.   160

DON PEDRO: I would she had bestowed this dotage on me. I would have daffed all other respects and made her half myself. I pray you tell Benedick of it, and hear what 'a will say.

LEONATO: Were it good think you?

CLAUDIO: Hero thinks surely she will die; for she says she

169   *bate*, abate. *crossness*, perversity.
170   *tender*, offer.

172   *contemptible*, scornful.
173   *proper man*, fine figure of a man.
174   *hath ... happiness*, is fortunate in a good appearance.

176–7 *some ... wit.* Is this a jibe or cautious understatement?
177   *wit*, intelligence, understanding.

179   *Hector.* A son of Priam, king of Troy, the outstanding Trojan
       hero. He was killed by Achilles.

187   *howsoever*, although, however much. *large*, broad, coarse.

190–1 *wear ... counsel*, endure it with wise determination.
191   *counsel*, determination.
192–3 *wear ... out.* The heart was the source of good counsel (see *Corio-*
       lanus, I.i.120). A quibble on 'wear out'.

198   *Dinner.* A midday meal. In l. 34 the time is evening.

200   *expectation*, powers of anticipation.

94

will die, if he love her not; and she will die ere she make her love known; and she will die if he woo her, rather than she will bate one breath of her accustomed crossness.

DON PEDRO: She doth well. If she should make tender of her love, 'tis very possible he'll scorn it; for the man, as you know all, hath a contemptible spirit.　172

CLAUDIO: He is a very proper man.

DON PEDRO: He hath indeed a good outward happiness.

CLAUDIO: Before God, and in my mind, very wise.

DON PEDRO: He doth indeed show some sparks that are like wit.

CLAUDIO: And I take him to be valiant.

DON PEDRO: As Hector, I assure you; and in the managing of quarrels you may say he is wise, for either he avoids them with great discretion, or undertakes them with a most Christian-like fear.　182

LEONATO: If he do fear God, 'a must necessarily keep peace; if he break the peace, he ought to enter into a quarrel with fear and trembling.

DON PEDRO: And so will he do; for the man doth fear God, howsoever it seems not in him by some large jests he will make. Well, I am sorry for your niece. Shall we go seek Benedick, and tell him of her love?

CLAUDIO: Never tell him, my lord; let her wear it out with good counsel.　191

LEONATO: Nay that's impossible, she may wear her heart out first.

DON PEDRO: Well, we will hear further of it by your daughter; let it cool the while. I love Benedick well, and I could wish he would modestly examine himself, to see how much he is unworthy so good a lady.

LEONATO: My lord, will you walk? Dinner is ready.

CLAUDIO: [Aside] If he do not dote on her upon this, I will never trust my expectation.　200

201   *net*, i.e. for a bird.

203   *carry*, carry out.
203-4   *they ... dotage*, they each hold a like opinion of the other's infatua-
        tion.
205-6   *merely ... show*, an absolutely speechless spectacle, a complete pan-
        tomime.

208   *sadly borne*, seriously carried on.

210   *have ... bent*, are stretched to the uttermost (like a bow).

216-18 *They ... me*. See ll. 24-5.
217   *reprove*, deny.
218-19 *no ... wit*, adds nothing to her wisdom, or, is no enhancement
        of her intelligence.
219   *argument*, proof.
220   *horribly*, exceedingly.
221   *odd quirks*, sarcastic cracks. *remnants of wit*, witticisms, banter,
        cracks. *broken on me*, thrown at me, at my expense.

224   *quips*, sharp sayings. *sentences*, proverbs.
225   *paper ... brain*, flimsy sallies of wit.
226   *career ... humour*, following the bent of his desires.

DON PEDRO: [*To Leonato*] Let there be the same net spread for her, and that must your daughter and her gentle-women carry. The sport will be, when they hold one an opinion of another's dotage, and no such matter. That's the scene that I would see, which will be merely a dumb show. Let us send her to call him in to dinner.   206

[*Exeunt Don Pedro, Claudio, and Leonato*

BENEDICK: [*Comes forward*] This can be no trick. The conference was sadly borne. They have the truth of this from Hero. They seem to pity the lady. It seems her affections have their full bent. Love me? Why, it must be requited. I hear how I am censured: they say I will bear myself proudly, if I perceive the love come from her; they say too that she will rather die than give any sign of affection. I did never think to marry. I must not seem proud. Happy are they that hear their detractions and can put them to mending. They say the lady is fair; 'tis a truth, I can bear them witness; and virtuous; so, I cannot reprove it; and wise, but for loving me. By my troth, it is no addition to her wit, nor no great argument of her folly, for I will be horribly in love with her. I may chance have some odd quirks and remnants of wit broken on me, because I have railed so long against marriage. But doth not the appetite alter? A man loves the meat in his youth that he cannot endure in his age. Shall quips and sentences, and these paper bullets of the brain awe a man from the career of his humour? No, the world must be peopled. When I said I would die a bachelor, I did not think I should live till I were married. Here comes Beatrice. By this day, she's a fair lady. I do spy some marks of love in her.   230

Enter BEATRICE

BEATRICE: Against my will I am sent to bid you come in to dinner.

233   *Fair ... pains.* Verse line. Should it be emphasized by Benedick
       as a sign of his love.

239   *daw*, fool.
240   *stomach*, (a) appetite, (b) zest for wit exchanges. Is this anything
       of a dumb show? See ll. 205–6.

242   *there's ... that.* Is there?

246   *Jew*, i.e. without Christian love.

       Benedick's reflections on the curious effects of falling in love are
       ironic in view of the trap in store for him. Some dramatic irony
       follows in the conspirators' conversation, where Benedick hears
       both truths and untruths about Beatrice, and learns some truths
       about himself. He makes virtue of his turn-about by claiming to
       show pity on the lady, by renouncing pride, and by acknowledg-
       ing Beatrice's virtues. As a defence against mockery and a justifica-
       tion for his change of heart, he cites a proverb exemplifying
       change, the fulfilling of social obligations, and a pretty twist of
       intent with 'die a bachelor' and 'live till I were married'.

BENEDICK: Fair Beatrice, I thank you for your pains.

BEATRICE: I took no more pains for those thanks than you take pains to thank me. If it had been painful, I would not have come.

BENEDICK: You take pleasure then in the message?   237

BEATRICE: Yea, just so much as you may take upon a knife's point, and choke a daw withal. You have no stomach signor; fare you well.   [*Exit*

BENEDICK: Ha! 'Against my will I am sent to bid you come in to dinner' – there's a double meaning in that. 'I took no more pains for those thanks than you took pains to thank me' – that's as much as to say, 'Any pains that I take for you is as easy as thanks'. If I do not take pity of her, I am a villain; if I do not love her, I am a Jew. I will go get her picture.   [*Exit*

99

Leonato's orchard

3   *Proposing*, talking.

7   *pleached bower*, an arbour made of interwoven branches of honey-
     suckle used earlier by Benedick.
8–11 *Where ... it.* The sun was the emblem of a king. This image of
     ingratitude and pride occurs elsewhere in Shakespeare: *Richard
     II*, III.iv.29–35; *The Tempest*, I.ii.80–1. Has the image any bearing
     on the attitudes of Benedick and Beatrice?
10   *advance*, thrust forward, flaunt. *pride*, insolence.
12   *propose*, conversation. *office*, task.
14   *presently*, immediately.

16   *trace*, tread, pace. *alley*, path.

23   *That ... hearsay*, that inspires love solely by the favourable
     comments of others.

100

ACT THREE

SCENE ONE

Enter HERO, MARGARET, *and* URSULA

HERO: Good Margaret, run thee to the parlour;
  There shalt thou find my cousin Beatrice
  Proposing with the Prince and Claudio.
  Whisper her ear, and tell her I and Ursula
  Walk in the orchard, and our whole discourse
  Is all of her. Say that thou overheardst us,
  And bid her steal into the pleached bower,
  Where honeysuckles, ripened by the sun,
  Forbid the sun to enter – like favourites,
  Made proud by princes, that advance their pride   10
  Against that power that bred it. There will she hide her
  To listen our propose. This is thy office;
  Bear thee well in it, and leave us alone.
MARGARET: I'll make her come, I warrant you, presently.
                                           [*Exit*

HERO: Now Ursula, when Beatrice doth come,
  As we do trace this alley up and down,
  Our talk must only be of Benedick.
  When I do name him, let it be thy part
  To praise him more than ever man did merit.
  My talk to thee must be how Benedick   20
  Is sick in love with Beatrice. Of this matter
  Is little Cupid's crafty arrow made,
  That only wound by hearsay. Now begin;

24–5   *like . . . ground.* An apt image, even more apt if Beatrice was dressed
        in black and white. The lapwing makes short bursts of rapid run-
        ning, then pauses to look around and listen.

30   *couched*, hiding.

35   *coy*, aloof, scornful.
        Should Beatrice react in any way during this scene?
36   *haggards.* A haggard was a female hawk that had been free and
        was considered almost untrainable. *of the rock*, i.e. a peregrine fal-
        con.

45–6   *as . . . upon*, quite as prosperous a marriage as he would make with
        Beatrice, or, as good a wife as Beatrice?

48   *As . . . man*, i.e. a woman's love. Benedick has all the manly virtues
        (see II.iii.173–88).

51   *Disdain . . . eyes.* This may owe something to an emblem picture.
        Spenser, *Faerie Queene*, VI.vii.27–44, depicts proud and 'coy'
        Mirabella as riding on horse led by a churlish fellow (disdain) and
        a fool (scorn).

Act Three, Scene One

Enter BEATRICE *into the bower*

    For look where Beatrice like a lapwing runs
    Close by the ground, to hear our conference.
URSULA: The pleasant'st angling is to see the fish
    Cut with her golden oars the silver stream,
    And greedily devour the treacherous bait.
    So angle we for Beatrice, who even now
    Is couched in the woodbine coverture.   30
    Fear you not my part of the dialogue.
HERO: Then go we near her, that her ear lose nothing
    Of the false sweet bait that we lay for it.
                          [*They approach the bower*
    No truly Ursula, she is too disdainful.
    I know her spirits are as coy and wild
    As haggards of the rock.
URSULA: But are you sure
    That Benedick loves Beatrice so entirely?
HERO: So says the Prince and my new-trothed lord.
URSULA: And did they bid you tell her of it, madam?
HERO: They did entreat me to acquaint her of it;   40
    But I persuaded them, if they loved Benedick,
    To wish him wrestle with affection,
    And never to let Beatrice know of it.
URSULA: Why did you so? Doth not the gentleman
    Deserve as full as fortunate a bed
    As ever Beatrice shall couch upon?
HERO: O god of love! I know he doth deserve
    As much as may be yielded to a man;
    But nature never framed a woman's heart
    Of prouder stuff than that of Beatrice.   50
    Disdain and scorn ride sparkling in her eyes,

52   *Misprizing*, despising.

54   *All ... weak*, all other subjects of conversation seem worthless.
55   *take ... affection*, accept love in any conceivable form.
56   *so self-endeared*, so full of self-love.

60   *How*, however. *rarely featured*, exceptionally handsome.
61   *spell him backward*, make his good qualities appear as bad ones.
      See V.i.153–63 where Beatrice 'did ... trans-shape thy particular
      virtues'.
63   *black*, swarthy. *antic*, grotesque creature.

65   *agate ... cut*, mis-shaped man carved on an agate. Such cameos
      were often set in seal rings.
66   *vane ... winds*, i.e. an idle gossip.

70   *simpleness*, uprightness, honesty. *purchaseth*, earn, deserve.
71   *carping*, fault-finding.
72   *from*, out of keeping with.

75   *mock ... air*, reduce my words to empty air.
76   *press ... wit*. Allusion to the torture *peine forte et dure*, popularly
      called 'pressing to death', in which weights were placed on a
      prisoner's chest to compel him to plead. If he failed to plead, he
      was crushed to death. Is there a pun, 'wit'/'weight'?
77   *covered*, either, banked down, or, covered with an iron plate.
      Don Pedro, Claudio, and Leonato think that Benedick will scorn
      Beatrice's love; Hero dares not mention to Beatrice Benedick's
      love for her lest she should be mocked out of countenance.

84   *honest slanders*. Oxymoron. *honest*, harmless.

Misprizing what they look on, and her wit
Values itself so highly that to her
All matter else seems weak. She cannot love,
Nor take no shape nor project of affection,
She is so self-endeared.

URSULA: Sure I think so,
And therefore certainly it were not good
She knew his love, lest she'll make sport at it.

HERO: Why, you speak truth. I never yet saw man,
How wise, how noble, young, how rarely featured,   60
But she would spell him backward. If fair-faced,
She would swear the gentleman should be her sister;
If black, why, Nature, drawing of an antic,
Made a foul blot; if tall, a lance ill-headed;
If low, an agate very vilely cut;
If speaking, why, a vane blown with all winds;
If silent, why, a block moved with none.
So turns she every man the wrong side out,
And never gives to truth and virtue that
Which simpleness and merit purchaseth.   70

URSULA: Sure, sure, such carping is not commendable.

HERO: No, not to be so odd and from all fashions
As Beatrice is, cannot be commendable.
But who dare tell her so? If I should speak,
She would mock me into air; o she would laugh me
Out of myself, press me to death with wit.
Therefore let Benedick, like covered fire,
Consume away in sighs, waste inwardly.
It were a better death than die with mocks,
Which is as bad as die with tickling.   80

URSULA: Yet tell her of it, hear what she will say.

HERO: No, rather I will go to Benedick,
And counsel him to fight against his passion.
And truly I'll devise some honest slanders

85–6   *One . . . liking*. Irony in Hero's ignorance of the plot against herself.

90   *prized*, esteemed.

92   *only*, without equal.

96   *argument and valour*. Argument may mean skill in reasoning, but
       the phrase may be a hendiadys and be rendered 'of proven valour',
       or 'theme of valour'. (See 'theme of honour's tongue', *I Henry
       IV*, I.i.81.)

101   *every day, tomorrow*, in my imagination every day – actually
       tomorrow. Hero's eagerness bubbles over.
102   *attires*, head-dresses.
103   *is . . . me*, will best become me.
104   *limed*, caught. Bird-lime was a sticky substance smeared on twigs
       to catch small birds.
105   *haps*, chance.

107   *What . . . ears?* Proverbially your ears burn when others talk of
       you.

110   *No . . . such*, i.e. such a person is condemned behind her back.

113   *incite*, urge.

To stain my cousin with. One doth not know
How much an ill word may empoison liking.

URSULA: O do not do your cousin such a wrong.
She cannot be so much without true judgment –
Having so swift and excellent a wit
As she is prized to have – as to refuse   90
So rare a gentleman as Signor Benedick.

HERO: He is the only man of Italy,
Always excepted my dear Claudio.

URSULA: I pray you be not angry with me, madam,
Speaking my fancy, Signor Benedick,
For shape, for bearing, argument and valour,
Goes foremost in report through Italy.

HERO: Indeed he hath an excellent good name.

URSULA: His excellence did earn it ere he had it..
When are you married, madam?   100

HERO: Why, every day, tomorrow. Come, go in.
I'll show thee some attires, and have thy counsel
Which is the best to furnish me tomorrow.

URSULA: [*Aside*] She's limed I warrant you; we have caught
her, madam.

HERO: [*Aside*] If it proves so, then loving goes by haps;
Some Cupid kills with arrows, some with traps.
                                    [*Exeunt Hero and Ursula*

BEATRICE: [*Comes forward*] What fire is in mine ears? Can
this be true?
Stand I condemned for pride and scorn so much?
Contempt, farewell; and maiden pride, adieu.
No glory lives behind the back of such.   110
And Benedick, love on; I will requite thee,
Taming my wild heart to thy loving hand.
If thou dost love, my kindness shall incite thee
To bind our loves up in a holy band.

116   *reportingly*, by hearsay.

The scene is in verse throughout – why?
The rhymes of Beatrice's speech add a seal of sincerity to her words. Beatrice, unlike Benedick, makes no comment while she is eavesdropping. She accepts and acts on what she has heard with warmth and dignity. Benedick argues himself into requiting love with sprightly wit and dubious logic – a figure of fun.

Leonato's house

3–4   *I'll ... me.* Is Claudio – courteous, grateful, zealous, deeply friendly towards Don Pedro, unenthusiastic about his bride?

3   *bring*, escort, accompany.

3–4   *vouchsafe*, permit.

6   *gloss*, brightness. Used of new clothes.

6–7   *child ... it.* Juliet's impatience (*Romeo and Juliet*, III.ii.28–31) has the same comparison.

7   *only ... with*, venture to ask only.

8–9   *from ... mirth.* Unconsciously ironic. Benedick is now a serious, sighing lover with a solemn face.

10   *cut Cupid's bow-string*, disarmed Cupid. *hangman*, rogue.

15   *sadder*, more serious.

17   *Hang him truant*, hang him as a truant from love.

22   *Hang it.* This may be an exclamation of annoyance or pain. But the barber-surgeons who extracted teeth hung them up in their windows.

For others say thou dost deserve, and I
Believe it better than reportingly.

[*Exit*

SCENE TWO

Enter DON PEDRO, CLAUDIO, BENEDICK, *and* LEONATO

DON PEDRO: I do but stay till your marriage be consummate, and then go I toward Arragon.

CLAUDIO: I'll bring you thither my lord, if you'll vouchsafe me.

DON PEDRO: Nay, that would be as great a soil in the new gloss of your marriage as to show a child his new coat and forbid him to wear it. I will only be bold with Benedick for his company; for from the crown of his head to the sole of his foot he is all mirth. He hath twice or thrice cut Cupid's bow-string, and the little hangman dare not shoot at him. He hath a heart as sound as a bell and his tongue is the clapper, for what his heart thinks, his tongue speaks.   13

BENEDICK: Gallants, I am not as I have been.

LEONATO: So say I, methinks you are sadder.

CLAUDIO: I hope he be in love.

DON PEDRO: Hang him truant. There's no true drop of blood in him to be truly touched with love. If he be sad, he wants money.

BENEDICK: I have the toothache.   20

DON PEDRO: Draw it.

BENEDICK: Hang it.

23   *You ... afterwards*, i.e. as a condemned man was hanged, drawn, and quartered. *draw*, (a) pull, (b) disembowel.
25   *humour*, pus. *worm*, maggot.
26–7 *everyone ... it.* Proverbial.
26   *grief*, pain.

29   *fancy*, love.
30   *fancy*, whim, liking.
30–4 *strange ... doublet.* Englishmen of fashion were often satirized for their indiscriminate copying of foreign fashions in clothes. See *The Merchant of Venice*, I.ii.62–5.
30   *strange*, (a) foreign, (b) queer.
33   *slops*, baggy breeches.
34–6 *Unless ... is.* Antimetabole, and a repetitive play on 'appears he hath' and 'appear he is'.
34   *fancy*, inclination.
35   *fancy*, love.
39   *bode*, signify.

42   *old ... cheek*, his beard, which makes him look old.
42–3 *hath ... tennis-balls.* Balls for the game of real tennis were made of leather stuffed with hair.
44–5 *Indeed ... beard.* Beatrice has no wish for an old husband with a beard nor an immature youth (II.i.26–7, 32–4).
46   *civet*, a musky perfume derived from the civet cat.
46–7 *smell ... that*, (a) discover his secret, (b) locate him.
48   *sweet*, (a) charming, (b) sweet-smelling.

51   *wont*, accustomed. *wash his face*, i.e. a barber's washing with scented lather.
52   *paint*, apply lotions.
54–5 *crept ... lute-string*, i.e. his vivacity has now become melancholy and is expressed by love songs to the lute.
55   *now ... stops*, i.e. his thought is no longer free and uninhibited. *stops*, (a) pauses, (b) frets – rings of gut, regulating the fingering on a lute.

CLAUDIO: You must hang it first, and draw it afterwards.

DON PEDRO: What? Sigh for the toothache?

LEONATO: Where is but a humour or a worm.

BENEDICK: Well, everyone can master a grief but he that has it.

CLAUDIO: Yet say I, he is in love. 28

DON PEDRO: There is no appearance of fancy in him, unless it be a fancy that he hath to strange disguises; as to be a Dutchman today, a Frenchman tomorrow, or in the shape of two countries at once, as, a German from the waist downward, all slops, and a Spaniard from the hip upward, no doublet. Unless he have a fancy to this foolery, as it appears he hath, he is no fool for fancy, as you would have it appear he is.

CLAUDIO: If he be not in love with some woman, there is no believing old signs. 'A brushes his hat o'morning; what should that bode?

DON PEDRO: Hath any man seen him at the barber's? 40

CLAUDIO: No, but the barber's man hath been seen with him, and the old ornament of his cheek hath already stuffed tennis-balls.

LEONATO: Indeed he looks younger than he did, by the loss of a beard.

DON PEDRO: Nay 'a rubs himself with civet; can you smell him out by that?

CLAUDIO: That's as much as to say, the sweet youth's in love.

DON PEDRO: The greatest note of it is his melancholy. 50

CLAUDIO: And when was he wont to wash his face?

DON PEDRO: Yea, or to paint himself? For the which I hear what they say of him.

CLAUDIO: Nay but his jesting spirit, which is now crept into a lute-string, and now governed by stops.

56   *heavy*, sad.

61   *ill conditions*, bad qualities.
62   *dies*, pines away.

64   *Old*, honoured.

66   *hobby-horses*, jokers, clowns. The figure of a horse made of canvas and wood was fastened to the waist of a morris dancer, who performed horse-like antics.
68   *break with*, formally ask.
70-1   *two ... meet*, i.e. Benedick and Beatrice. Proverbially 'one bear will not bite another'.

74   *your leisure served*, you have a moment to spare.

83   *impediment*. An echo of the Banns and the Marriage Service. *discover*, reveal.
85   *You ... not*. Is this–hypocrisy, irony, sarcasm?
86   *aim ... me*, hold a better opinion of me.
87   *holds you well*, regards you highly.

DON PEDRO : Indeed that tells a heavy tale for him; conclude, conclude he is in love.

CLAUDIO : Nay but I know who loves him.

DON PEDRO : That would I know too. I warrant one that knows him not.   60

CLAUDIO : Yes, and his ill conditions; and in despite of all dies for him.

DON PEDRO : She shall be buried with her face upwards.

BENEDICK : Yet is this no charm for the toothache. Old signor, walk aside with me; I have studied eight or nine wise words to speak to you, which these hobby-horses must not hear.   [*Exeunt Benedick and Leonato*

DON PEDRO : For my life, to break with him about Beatrice.

CLAUDIO : 'Tis even so. Hero and Margaret have by this played their parts with Beatrice, and then the two bears will not bite one another when they meet.   71

Enter DON JOHN

DON JOHN : My lord and brother, God save you.

DON PEDRO : Good-e'en, brother.

DON JOHN : If your leisure served, I would speak with you.

DON PEDRO : In private?

DON JOHN : If it please you, yet Count Claudio may hear, for what I would speak of concerns him.

DON PEDRO : What's the matter?

DON JOHN : [*To Claudio*] Means your lordship to be married tomorrow?   80

DON PEDRO : You know he does.

DON JOHN : I know not that, when he knows what I know.

CLAUDIO : If there be an impediment, I pray you discover it.

DON JOHN : You may think I love you not; let that appear hereafter, and aim better at me by that I now will manifest. For my brother, I think he holds you well, and in dearness

113

87–8 *dearness of heart*, affection.
88 *holp*, helped.
89 *suit*, courtship. *ill spent*, wasted.

91–2 *circumstances shortened*, leaving out the details.

98 *paint out*, describe fully.

101 *warrant*, evidence.

111–15 *If... her.* Are Claudio and Don Pedro – savage, bitter, just, cold, calculating, enraged, dishonoured, credulous, selfish? Do they react by gesture or movement?

117 *Bear it coldly*, control your feelings, keep cool.

119 *untowardly turned*, turned to misery.
120 *O ... thwarting*, o wrong, utterly thwarting everything.

of heart hath holp to effect your ensuing marriage – surely
suit ill spent, and labour ill bestowed.

DON PEDRO: Why, what's the matter? 90

DON JOHN: I came hither to tell you; and, circumstances
shortened – for she has been too long a talking of – the
lady is disloyal.

CLAUDIO: Who, Hero?

DON JOHN: Even she, Leonato's Hero, your Hero, every
man's Hero.

CLAUDIO: Disloyal?

DON JOHN: The word is too good to paint out her wicked-
ness. I could say she were worse; think you of a worse
title, and I will fit her to it. Wonder not till further
warrant. Go but with me tonight, you shall see her
chamber-window entered, even the night before her
wedding-day. If you love her then, tomorrow wed her;
but it would better fit your honour to change your mind.

CLAUDIO: May this be so? 105

DON PEDRO: I will not think it.

DON JOHN: If you dare not trust that you see, confess not
that you know. If you will follow me, I will show you
enough; and when you have seen more and heard more,
proceed accordingly.

CLAUDIO: If I see any thing tonight why I should not marry
her tomorrow, in the congregation, where I should wed,
there will I shame her. 113

DON PEDRO: And as I wooed for thee to obtain her, I will
join with thee to disgrace her.

DON JOHN: I will disparage her no farther till you are my
witness. Bear it coldly but till midnight, and let the issue
show itself.

DON PEDRO: O day untowardly turned!

CLAUDIO: O mischief strangely thwarting! 120

The scene moves from the complacent confidence of Don Pedro and Claudio in the marriage arrangements, the touch of irony that its 'new gloss' should not be soiled, the mocking of Benedick, to the misery of their belief in Don John's accusations, a complete change in the direction of the romantic plot.

A street near a church

A church bench is required. Should the Watch have lanterns or torches?

S.D.   *Dogberry*, it has been suggested, is round and rubicund like the hips of the dog-rose or the berries of the mountain ash. *Verges*. The name may be derived from 'verge', a rod or staff, or 'ver-juice', acid, unripe fruit juice, or both. Should he be lean, tall, sour-faced, or a tipstaff? *Watch*, company of men armed with pikes, bills, or halberds who patrolled the city streets at night.

1   *Are ... true*, i.e. have no criminal record.

3   *salvation*, i.e. damnation. In spite of the gift of these two for using words opposite in meaning to what they intend, lucidity occasionally breaks through.

5   *allegiance*, i.e. disloyalty. As officers of the crown they would have sworn allegiance to the king.

7   *charge*, instructions.

9   *desartless*, i.e. deserving.

10   *constable*, Dogberry's deputy for the night.

11   *Hugh ... Seacoal*, perhaps dealers in oatcakes and sea coal. Sea coal was gathered particularly on the north-east sea-shore from seams exposed by the waves.

14–16   *To ... nature*. Which gifts were bestowed by nature and which by fortune was much discussed. See *As You Like It*, I.ii.25–46.

14   *well-favoured*, handsome.

16   *nature*, i.e. nurture. See *The Tempest*, IV.i.188–9.

DON JOHN: O plague right well prevented! So will you say when you have seen the sequel.

[*Exeunt*

SCENE THREE

Enter DOGBERRY *and his compartner* VERGES
with the WATCH

DOGBERRY: Are you good men and true?

VERGES: Yea, or else it were pity but they should suffer salvation, body and soul.

DOGBERRY: Nay, that were a punishment too good for them, if they should have any allegiance in them, being chosen for the Prince's watch.

VERGES: Well, give them their charge, neighbour Dogberry.

DOGBERRY: First, who think you the most desartless man to be constable? 10

FIRST WATCHMAN: Hugh Oatcake sir, or George Seacoal, for they can write and read.

DOGBERRY: Come hither neighbour Seacoal. God hath blessed you with a good name. To be a well-favoured man is the gift of fortune, but to write and read comes by nature.

SECOND WATCHMAN: Both which, Master Constable–

DOGBERRY: You have. I knew it would be your answer. Well, for your favour sir, why, give God thanks, and make no boast of it; and for your writing and reading, let that appear when there is no need of such vanity. You are thought here to be the most senseless and fit man for the constable of the watch; therefore bear you the lantern. This

24   *comprehend*, i.e. apprehend. *vagrom*, vagrant.

25   *stand*, stop.

32   *meddle with*, interfere with, have to do with.

33–7 *You ... watch*. Both were common complaints about the watch.

35   *tolerable*, i.e. intolerable.

38   *ancient*, of long service, veteran.

40   *bills*, spears with an axe-head attached below the spearhead.

49   *true*, honest.

50   *meddle or make*. Proverbial phrase. *make*, have to do.

53   *lay hands on*, (a) arrest, (b) touch.

54–5 *they ... defiled*. Proverbial. See *Ecclus.*, xiii.1.

57   *steal*. Any response to this pun?

is your charge: you shall comprehend all vagrom men; you
are to bid any man stand, in the Prince's name.   25

SECOND WATCHMAN: How if 'a will not stand?

DOGBERRY: Why then take no note of him, but let him go;
and presently call the rest of the watch together, and thank
God you are rid of a knave.

VERGES: If he will not stand when he is bidden, he is none
of the Prince's subjects.

DOGBERRY: True, and they are to meddle with none but the
Prince's subjects. You shall also make no noise in the
streets; for, for the watch to babble and to talk is most
tolerable and not to be endured.

FIRST WATCHMAN: We will rather sleep than talk; we
know what belongs to a watch.

DOGBERRY: Why you speak like an ancient and most quiet
watchman, for I cannot see how sleeping should offend.
Only have a care that your bills be not stolen. Well, you
are to call at all the ale-houses, and bid those that are drunk
get them to bed.   42

SECOND WATCHMAN: How if they will not?

DOGBERRY: Why then let them alone till they are sober.
If they make you not then the better answer, you may
say they are not the men you took them for.

SECOND WATCHMAN: Well, sir.

DOGBERRY: If you meet a thief, you may suspect him, by
virtue of your office, to be no true man; and for such
kind of men, the less you meddle or make with them,
why, the more is for your honesty.   51

SECOND WATCHMAN: If we know him to be a thief, shall
we not lay hands on him?

DOGBERRY: Truly by your office you may, but I think they
that touch pitch will be defiled. The most peaceable way
for you, if you do take a thief, is to let him show himself
what he is, and steal out of your company.

68-9   *will ... bleats*, i.e. the watchman when he calls! Dogberry's attempt at a proverb has a telling misapplication.

72   *present*, represent.

76   *statutes*, laws. F reading 'statues' is adopted by some editors as a likely Dogberrian misuse.

77-8   *the ... man*. This sums up the theme of the charge – to avoid doing what they ought to do for fear of giving offence or of committing an offence.

81   *Ha, ah ha*, got you there!

82-3   *Keep ... own*. An off-beat version of the proverb, 'The counsel thou wouldest have another keep, first keep thyself'.

90   *coil*, ado, bustle.

91   *vigitant*, i.e. vigilant.

VERGES: You have been always called a merciful man, partner.

DOGBERRY: Truly I would not hang a dog by my will, much more a man who hath any honesty in him.   61

VERGES: If you hear a child cry in the night, you must call to the nurse and bid her still it.

SECOND WATCHMAN: How if the nurse be asleep and will not hear us?

DOGBERRY: Why then depart in peace, and let the child wake her with crying; for the ewe that will not hear her lamb when it baes, will never answer a calf when he bleats.

VERGES: 'Tis very true.   70

DOGBERRY: This is the end of the charge. You constable are to present the Prince's own person; if you meet the Prince in the night, you may stay him.

VERGES: Nay by'r lady that I think 'a cannot.

DOGBERRY: Five shillings to one on't with any man that knows the statutes, he may stay him; marry not without the Prince be willing; for indeed the watch ought to offend no man, and it is an offence to stay a man against his will.

VERGES: By'r lady I think it be so.   80

DOGBERRY: Ha, ah ha! Well masters good night. An there be any matter of weight chances, call up me. Keep your fellows' counsels and your own, and good night. Come neighbour.

FIRST WATCHMAN: Well masters, we hear our charge. Let us go sit here upon the church-bench till two, and then all go to bed.

DOGBERRY: One word more, honest neighbours. I pray you watch about Signor Leonato's door, for the wedding being there tomorrow, there is a great coil tonight. Adieu, be vigitant I beseech you.   [*Exeunt Dogberry and Verges*

S.D. The name Borachio may be derived from a Spanish word for drunkard. Here he is slightly fuddled, groping in the dark and not quite sure where Conrade is.

96–7 *Mass ... follow*. Itching of the elbow was thought to foretell a change of fortune. Borachio takes the itching literally.

96 *Mass*, the Roman Catholic Eucharist service, here used as an oath.

97 *scab*, (a) dried blood of a wound, (b) rogue.

100 *pent-house*, projecting roof. Perhaps the canopy or 'heaven' of an Elizabethan stage. How are the characters grouped?

101–2 *like ... thee*. Proverbially 'a man being overseen with wine doth utter the secrets of his mind'.

103 *treason*, villainy.

104 *stand close*, keep hidden.

106 *ducats*. A ducat, originally Sicilian, was a gold or silver coin of varying value in general use in Europe.

112 *unconfirmed*, ignorant, inexperienced.

114 *is ... man*, (a) does not proclaim the real man, (b) is of no consequence when compared with a man.

115 *it is apparel*, it is of no importance, just clothes.

119 *what ... is*, i.e. it steals away a man's true appearance.

120–2 *I ... name*. There may be a glance at the Devil (see l. 147), sometimes described as ugly, or deformed and as a gentleman (*King Lear*, III.iv.148; IV.ii.59–60). In the morality play, *All for Money* (1578), 'Satan the great devil' comes on stage 'as deformedly dressed as may be'.

Enter BORACHIO *and* CONRADE

BORACHIO: What, Conrade!

SECOND WATCHMAN: [*Aside*] Peace, stir not.

BORACHIO: Conrade I say!

CONRADE: Here man, I am at thy elbow.

BORACHIO: Mass, and my elbow itched, I thought there would a scab follow.

CONRADE: I will owe thee an answer for that, and now forward with thy tale.   99

BORACHIO: Stand thee close then under this pent-house, for it drizzles rain, and I will, like a true drunkard, utter all to thee.

SECOND WATCHMAN: [*Aside*] Some treason masters; yet stand close.

BORACHIO: Therefore know I have earned of Don John a thousand ducats.

CONRADE: Is it possible that any villainy should be so dear?

BORACHIO: Thou shouldst rather ask if it were possible any villainy should be so rich. For when rich villains have need of poor ones, poor ones may make what price they will.

CONRADE: I wonder at it.   111

BORACHIO: That shows thou art unconfirmed. Thou knowest that the fashion of a doublet, or a hat, or a cloak, is nothing to a man.

CONRADE: Yes, it is apparel.

BORACHIO: I mean the fashion.

CONRADE: Yes, the fashion is the fashion.

BORACHIO: Tush, I may as well say the fool's the fool. But seest thou not what a deformed thief this fashion is?   119

FIRST WATCHMAN: [*Aside*] I know that Deformed, 'a has been a vile thief this seven year, 'a goes up and down like a gentleman. I remember his name.

BORACHIO: Didst thou not hear somebody?

128   *Pharaoh's ... painting*. Perhaps a painting on tapestry or panel of
        the drowning of the Egyptian soldiers in the Red Sea (*Exod.*,
        xiv.23–8). *reechy*, smoky, dirty.
129   *god ... church-window*. In the story of Bel in the Apocrypha, his
        priests stole the food offered to the god but were detected by the
        young judge Daniel It is possible that the reference is to Elijah
        and the priests of Baal on Mount Carmel (*I Kings*, xviii). *old
        church-window*, i.e. stained glass that survived the Reformation
        (Harrison, *Description of Britain*).
130   *shaven Hercules*. Hercules was sometimes represented as beardless
        in painting and sculpture. It seems likely in representations of him
        as a slave to Queen Ompale who dressed him in woman's attire
        and made him spin and weave. *smirched*, smeared.
130–1   *worm-eaten*, moth-eaten.
131   *codpiece*, pouch in front of the breeches, often ornamented. The
        figures in the paintings would, according to custom, be depicted
        in contemporary sixteenth-century dress. Symbolic more of sex
        than strength.
135   *shifted*, (a) changed argument, (b) changed clothes.
137–9   *Not ... Hero*, i.e. Margaret has 'fashioned' herself like Hero. See
        V.i.224.
139   *me*. Personal pronouns are so used for emphasis, or, as the old
        dative and ablative cases. (See I.iii.55, 'comes me'.)
140–1   *I ... vilely*. How – in sequence of thought, enunciation, omission?
142   *planted*, possessed. Drunken plosion of p's. *possessed*, informed.
148   *oaths*, sworn information.

152   *temple*, church.

CONRADE: No, 'twas the vane on the house.

BORACHIO: Seest thou not, I say, what a deformed thief
this fashion is, how giddily 'a turns about all the hot bloods
between fourteen and five-and-thirty, sometimes fashioning them like Pharaoh's soldiers in the reechy painting,
sometime like god Bel's priests in the old church-window,
sometime like the shaven Hercules in the smirched worm-
eaten tapestry, where his codpiece seems as massy as his
club? 132

CONRADE: All this I see, and I see that the fashion wears out
more apparel than the man. But art not thou thyself giddy
with the fashion too, that thou hast shifted out of thy tale
into telling me of the fashion?

BORACHIO: Not so neither: but know that I have tonight
wooed Margaret, the Lady Hero's gentlewoman, by the
name of Hero. She leans me out at her mistress' chamber-
window, bids me a thousand times good night – I tell this
tale vilely – I should first tell thee how the Prince, Claudio,
and my master, planted and placed and possessed by my
master Don John, saw afar off in the orchard this amiable
encounter. 144

CONRADE: And thought they Margaret was Hero?

BORACHIO: Two of them did, the Prince and Claudio. But
the devil my master knew she was Margaret; and partly
by his oaths, which first possessed them, partly by the dark
night, which did deceive them, but chiefly by my villainy,
which did confirm any slander that Don John had made,
away went Claudio enraged; swore he would meet her as
he was appointed next morning at the temple, and there,
before the whole congregation, shame her with what he
saw o'er night, and send her home again without a
husband.

FIRST WATCHMAN: We charge you in the Prince's name,
stand!

158   *right*, right worthy. Title of address.
159   *recovered*, i.e. discovered.
160   *lechery*, i.e. treachery.

162   *lock*, curl, or lovelock worn at the ear (V.i.293). R. Greene's
      Defence of Coney-catching (1592) mentions disreputable swash-
      bucklers 'in the habit of gentlemen ... with a lock worn at their
      left ear for their mistress' favour'. Should Borachio wear a lock?

168   *obey*, order.
169-70 *goodly ... bills*, (a) notable prize arrested by these men's halberds,
      (b) valuable goods obtained by these bills of credit.
171   *in question*, (a) of questionable value, (b) subject to legal interroga-
      tion.

      The scene has a lively irony. The Watch, defenders of public
      order, so confusedly interpret their duty as to render themselves
      virtually incapable of arresting anybody. Borachio, promoter of
      disorder, in drunken confusion, declares his guilt, thus solving
      the Watch's problem. That he is charged with lechery brings
      down on his own head the same accusation that he had planted
      on Hero.

Leonato's house: Hero's room

      Suggest which stage properties are appropriate – dresses,
      garments, head-dresses, seats, etc.

6   *rebato*, a stiff, decorated collar.

10   *My ... another*. Is Hero – playful, irritable, excited, merry,
      snappy, on edge, melancholy?

SECOND WATCHMAN: Call up the right Master Constable.
We have here recovered the most dangerous piece of
lechery that ever was known in the commonwealth. 160
FIRST WATCHMAN: And one Deformed is one of them; I
know him, 'a wears a lock.
CONRADE: Masters, masters—
SECOND WATCHMAN: You'll be made bring Deformed
forth I warrant you.
CONRADE: Masters—
FIRST WATCHMAN: Never speak, we charge you; let us
obey you to go with us.
BORACHIO: We are like to prove a goodly commodity,
being taken up of these men's bills. 170
CONRADE: A commodity in question I warrant you. Come,
we'll obey you.

[*Exeunt*

SCENE FOUR

Enter HERO, *and* MARGARET, *and* URSULA

HERO: Good Ursula wake my cousin Beatrice, and desire
her to rise.
URSULA: I will lady.
HERO: And bid her come hither.
URSULA: Well. [*Exit*
MARGARET: Troth I think your other rebato were better.
HERO: No, pray thee good Meg, I'll wear this.
MARGARET: By my troth 's not so good, and I warrant your
cousin will say so. 9
HERO: My cousin's a fool, and thou art another. I'll wear
none but this.

12   *tire*, a head-dress made of wire and hair. *within*, i.e. in an inner room.

13   *thought*, shade, trifle.

14   *rare*, excellent.

16   *exceeds*, surpasses everything.

17   *nightgown*, dressing-gown. *in respect of*, by comparison with.

18   *cloth o'gold*, cloth woven wholly or partly of gold thread. *cuts*, slashes in the edge of the dress for ornament, or to reveal different coloured tissue beneath.

19   *down sleeves*, *side sleeves*, close-fitting sleeves, loose open sleeves.

19–20 *round underborne*, trimmed round the bottom edge.

20   *quaint*, dainty, elegant.

22–3 *God ... heavy*. A premonition, and a reminder to the audience of Claudio's intentions. See note to l. 10 above.

26–7 *Of ... beggar*. Echo of 'honourable estate' of the marriage service in the Book of Common Prayer and of St Paul's view that marriage is 'honourable among all men' (*Heb.*, xiii.4).

29   *saving your reverence*, excuse me for mentioning.

Margaret's argument is: Isn't marriage honourable for anyone. Isn't Claudio honourable anyway. You're so prudish you would have me apologize for using the word husband. You can't make me offend by misinterpreting my words. Is there any harm in heavier for a husband as long as it's the right husband.

29–30 *an ... speaking*. Proverbially 'there were no ill language if it were not ill taken'.

29   *an*, if.

33   *light*, immodest.

37   *sick tune*, ill mood, gloomy feeling.

39   *Clap's into*, let us strike up. *Light o'love*. A popular ballad tune.

39–40 *that ... burden*, that has no male part. There is a similar allusion to 'Light o'love' in *The Two Gentlemen of Verona*, I.ii.83–96.

40   *burden*, (a) chorus, (b) male part, bass, (c) solemnity, heaviness.

41   *Ye ... heels*, you are promiscuous enough to go to bed with any man. *light*, unchaste, 'light heeled'.

43   *barns*, (a) bairns, (b) granaries, storehouses.

MARGARET: I like the new tire within excellently, if the hair were a thought browner. And your gown's a most rare fashion i'faith. I saw the Duchess of Milan's gown that they praise so.

HERO: O that exceeds, they say.

MARGARET: By my troth's but a nightgown in respect of yours – cloth o'gold, and cuts, and laced with silver, set with pearls, down sleeves, side sleeves, and skirts, round underborne with a bluish tinsel; but for a fine, quaint, graceful, and excellent fashion, yours is worth ten on't.

HERO: God give me joy to wear it, for my heart is exceedingly heavy.   23

MARGARET: 'Twill be heavier soon by the weight of a man.

HERO: Fie upon thee, art not ashamed?

MARGARET: Of what, lady? Of speaking honourably? Is not marriage honourable in a beggar? Is not your lord honourable without marriage? I think you would have me say, 'saving your reverence, a husband'; an bad thinking do not wrest true speaking, I'll offend nobody. Is there any harm in 'the heavier for a husband'? None, I think, an it be the right husband and the right wife; otherwise 'tis light, and not heavy. Ask my Lady Beatrice else, here she comes.   34

Enter BEATRICE

HERO: Good morrow coz.

BEATRICE: Good morrow sweet Hero.

HERO: Why how now? Do you speak in the sick tune?

BEATRICE: I am out of all other tune, methinks.

MARGARET: Clap's into 'Light o' love'; that goes without a burden. Do you sing it, and I'll dance it.   40

BEATRICE: Ye light o'love, with your heels! Then if your husband have stables enough, you'll see he shall lack no barns.

44 *illegitimate construction*, illogical interpretation. *illegitimate*, (a) unlawful, untrue, (b) bastard.

44–5 *scorn ... heels*, spurn it, reject that with contempt.

47 *Heigh-ho*, (a) a sigh – in II.i.289 it was for a husband, (b) cry used to urge a horse or a hawk.

49 *H*, (a) ache, (b) aitch. Both pronounced 'aitch'.

50–1 *an ... star*, if you have not given up your determination not to marry there is no certainty left in the world.

50 *Turk*, infidel, without (Christian) faith.

52 *trow*, do you suppose.

53–4 *God ... desire*. Margaret ends the exchanges with a pious hope in words from *Psalm xxxvii.4* (*Prayer Book*) 'Delight thou in the Lord: and he shall give thee thy heart's desire'.

55 *are*, have.

57 *stuffed*, stuffy from a cold in the nose.

58 *A ... stuffed*, a virgin and pregnant.

61 *professed apprehension*, laid claim to wit.

62 *Ever ... it*, i.e. since Beatrice's gulling in the eavesdropping scene. Margaret makes obscure references to Beatrice's new mood throughout these exchanges.

62–3 *become me rarely*, suit me excellently.

64–5 *It ... cap*, there isn't much in sight, you should wear it in your cap (as a fool does his coxcomb, Dover Wilson).

66 *distilled*, essence of, spirit of.

66–7 *Carduus Benedictus*, the Blessed Thistle, cultivated in gardens for use against fevers and as a cordial.

67 *lay ... heart*, i.e. literally and metaphorically, the cordial and Benedick.

68 *qualm*, sudden faintness.

69 *There ... thistle*. Does Beatrice start suddenly at the mention of Carduus Benedictus as if pricked?

70–1 *Benedictus ... Benedictus*. Is Beatrice – suspicious, alert, wary, puzzled, calm, probing?

71 *moral*, hidden meaning.

72–81 *Moral ... grudging*. Margaret is deliberately confusing Beatrice, yet her general sense seems to be: whatever I wish and whatever I think I cannot allow myself to believe that you will fall in love. Yet Benedick has now grown up and in spite of his hard heart he is content.

75 *list*, please.

MARGARET: O illegitimate construction! I scorn that with my heels.

BEATRICE: 'Tis almost five o'clock cousin; 'tis time you were ready. By my troth I am exceeding ill. Heigh-ho!

MARGARET: For a hawk, a horse, or a husband?

BEATRICE: For the letter that begins them all, H.   49

MARGARET: Well, an you be not turned Turk, there's no more sailing by the star.

BEATRICE: What means the fool trow?

MARGARET: Nothing I; but God send everyone their heart's desire!

HERO: These gloves the Count sent me, they are an excellent perfume.

BEATRICE: I am stuffed, cousin, I cannot smell.

MARGARET: A maid, and stuffed! There's goodly catching of cold.   59

BEATRICE: O God help me, God help me, how long have you professed apprehension?

MARGARET: Ever since you left it. Doth not my wit become me rarely?

BEATRICE: It is not seen enough; you should wear it in your cap. By my troth I am sick.

MARGARET: Get you some of this distilled Carduus Benedictus, and lay it to your heart; it is the only thing for a qualm.

HERO: There thou prickest her with a thistle.   69

BEATRICE: Benedictus, why Benedictus? You have some moral in this Benedictus.

MARGARET: Moral? No by my troth I have no moral meaning; I meant plain holy-thistle. You may think perchance that I think you are in love. Nay by'r lady I am not such a fool to think what I list, nor I list not to think what I can, nor indeed I cannot think, if I would think my heart out of thinking, that you are in love, or that you will

82–3 *you ... eyes.* Love, it was held, entered through the eyes.
85 *false gallop,* (a) canter, (b) untrue discourse.
89 *Help ... Ursula.* A sudden flurry of excitement.

There is superb artistry in the construction of this scene. It opens with a natural conversation about wedding clothes but poised with irony and suspense over what has passed in the two previous scenes. The irony deepens and awakens a feeling of outrage as Hero reveals her delicate modesty. There is a reminder to the audience of the threat to Hero as she expresses a feeling of sadness. Attention is then diverted from Hero to Beatrice whose quickness of wit is for once slowed down. Beatrice is teased by Margaret who skates over very thin ice. Then with a sudden interruption the wedding with all its ambiguous outcome is upon them.

Leonato's house

Q reads 'Enter Leonato, and the Constable, and the Head-borough'. The Headborough was a kind of deputy constable.

1 *honest neighbour,* good friend.
2 *confidence,* i.e. conference.
3 *decerns,* i.e. concerns. *nearly,* closely.
4–5 *Brief ... me.* How could Leonato indicate his business in movement, gesture, or occupation?

9–10 *off the matter,* beside the point.

11–12 *honest ... brows.* Proverbial. The brow was thought to indicate honour, shame, and emotions (*Measure for Measure*, IV.ii.163; *I Henry IV*, I.i.85).

be in love, or that you can be in love. Yet Benedick was such another, and now is he become a man. He swore he would never marry, and yet now in despite of his heart he eats his meat without grudging. And how you may be converted, I know not, but methinks you look with your eyes as other women do. 83

BEATRICE: What pace is this that thy tongue keeps?

MARGARET: Not a false gallop.

Enter URSULA

URSULA: Madam withdraw; the Prince, the Count, Signor Benedick, Don John, and all the gallants of the town are come to fetch you to church.

HERO: Help to dress me good coz, good Meg, good Ursula.

[*Exeunt*

SCENE FIVE

Enter LEONATO, DOGBERRY, *and* VERGES

LEONATO: What would you with me, honest neighbour?

DOGBERRY: Marry sir, I would have some confidence with you that decerns you nearly.

LEONATO: Brief I pray you, for you see it is a busy time with me.

DOGBERRY: Marry this it is, sir.

VERGES: Yes in truth it is, sir.

LEONATO: What is it my good friends? 8

DOGBERRY: Goodman Verges sir speaks a little off the matter – an old man sir, and his wits are not so blunt as, God help, I would desire they were; but in faith honest as the skin between his brows.

15 *comparisons are odorous.* Bottom is also confused over 'odious' (*A Midsummer Night's Dream*, III.i.70). *palabras,* be brief. Part of a Spanish phrase 'pocas palabras', few words, formerly in use in England.

20 *tedious ... king.* From what follows Dogberry interprets 'tedious' as 'rich'. The proverb is 'rich as a king'.

24 *exclamation on,* clamour against. Perhaps Dogberry had in mind 'commendation' or 'report'.

28 *fain,* gladly.
29–30 *excepting ... presence.* Dogberry intends to apologize for mentioning such an unsavoury matter in Leonato's presence, but succeeds in classifying him as an arrant knave.

33–8 *When ... alike.* Dogberry, more than Verges, 'will be talking'. He rattles off a string of proverbs and popular truisms.
33 *When ... out.* Dogberry's version of 'when the ale is in the wit is out'.
33–4 *it ... see,* it is a marvellous thing to see.

39 *too ... you,* (a) smaller, (b) less voluble.

42–3 *comprehended,* i.e. apprehended.
43 *aspicious,* i.e. suspicious, confused with 'auspicious'.

VERGES: Yes I thank God, I am as honest as any man living that is an old man and no honester than I.

DOGBERRY: Comparisons are odorous – *palabras*, neighbour Verges.

LEONATO: Neighbours, you are tedious.

DOGBERRY: It pleases your worship to say so, but we are the poor Duke's officers. But truly for mine own part if I were as tedious as a king, I could find it in my heart to bestow it all of your worship.   21

LEONATO: All thy tediousness on me, ah?

DOGBERRY: Yea, an 'twere a thousand pound more than 'tis, for I hear as good exclamation on your worship as of any man in the city; and though I be but a poor man, I am glad to hear it.

VERGES: And so am I.

LEONATO: I would fain know what you have to say.

VERGES: Marry sir our watch tonight, excepting your worship's presence, ha' t'en a couple of as arrant knaves as any in Messina.   31

DOGBERRY: A good old man sir, he will be talking – as they say, 'When the age is in, the wit is out'. God help us, it is a world to see. Well said i'faith neighbour Verges. Well, God's a good man; an two men ride of a horse, one must ride behind. An honest soul i'faith sir, by my troth he is, as ever broke bread. But – God is to be worshipped – all men are not alike. Alas good neighbour!

LEONATO: Indeed neighbour he comes too short of you.

DOGBERRY: Gifts that God gives.   40

LEONATO: I must leave you.

DOGBERRY: One word sir: our watch sir, have indeed comprehended two aspicious persons, and we would have them this morning examined before your worship.

LEONATO: Take their examination yourself, and bring it me. I am now in great haste, as it may appear unto you.

47   *suffigance*, suffisance, i.e. sufficient. Dogberry perhaps means 'done with competence'.

48–51 *Drink ... ready.* Suspense, and exasperating irony at Dogberry's delays to Leonato's 'haste to the wedding'.

52–3   *Francis Seacoal.* His activities in IV.ii suggest that he is superior in calibre to George Seacoal (III.iii.11) even though the latter can read and write. Is this Shakespeare's carelessness or is it due to later alterations?

57   *that.* Indicates his own head. *non-come.* Short for 'non compos mentis', of unsound mind, but Dogberry perhaps means 'non-plus', quandary, corner.

58   *excommunication*, i.e. examination.

This brief scene, together with the previous one, most skilfully increases the tension, suspense, and dramatic irony. Is Leonato's haste here and at the beginning of the next scene an ironic reminder of 'marry in haste, repent at leisure'?

DOGBERRY: It shall be suffigance.

LEONATO: Drink some wine ere you go. Fare you well.

Enter a Messenger

MESSENGER: My lord, they stay for you to give your
daughter to her husband.   50

LEONATO: I'll wait upon them. I am ready.

[*Exeunt Leonato and Messenger*

DOGBERRY: Go good partner, go get you to Francis Seacoal, bid him bring his pen and inkhorn to the gaol. We
are now to examination these men.

VERGES: And we must do it wisely.

DOGBERRY: We will spare for no wit I warrant you. Here's
that shall drive some of them to a non-come; only get the
learned writer to set down our excommunication, and
meet me at the gaol.   [*Exeunt*

Inside church

A full ceremonial entry. Margaret is a notable absentee. Why? How should the participants be grouped? The properties would be limited, perhaps to candles, since an altar and crosses would almost certainly not have been allowed on stage.

1–3   *only . . . afterwards.* The Prayer Book service begins with an address on the purposes for which marriage was ordained and the obligations of the couple. Leonato asks that this be postponed.

10–11   *know . . . conjoined.* The words echo the Prayer Book service: 'join together', 'charge you', 'impediment', 'not be lawfully joined'.

16   *I . . . None.* Is Leonato's fussiness due to – age, anxiety, nervousness, excitement, pleasure, irritation, garrulity, indulgence of authority, his possible link with Father Time?

19–20 *How . . . he.* A joking reference to the section on interjections in Lily's *Latin Grammar*, the standard textbook. Benedick tries to enliven the proceedings.

21   *Stand thee by*, stand aside. *by your leave*, either, if I may call you by that name, or, with your permission (drawing him forward).

ACT FOUR

SCENE ONE

Enter DON PEDRO, DON JOHN, LEONATO,
FRIAR FRANCIS, CLAUDIO, BENEDICK, HERO,
BEATRICE, *and attendants*

LEONATO: Come Friar Francis, be brief; only to the plain
form of marriage, and you shall recount their particular
duties afterwards.

FRIAR: You come hither, my lord, to marry this lady?

CLAUDIO: No.

LEONATO: To be married to her. Friar, you come to marry
her.

FRIAR: Lady, you come hither to be married to this Count?

HERO: I do.   9

FRIAR: If either of you know any inward impediment why
you should not be conjoined, I charge you on your souls,
to utter it.

CLAUDIO: Know you any, Hero?

HERO: None my lord.

FRIAR: Know you any, Count?

LEONATO: I dare make his answer, None.

CLAUDIO: O what men dare do! What men may do!
What men daily do, not knowing what they do!

BENEDICK: How now, interjections? Why then, some be
of laughing, as, ah, ha, he!   20

CLAUDIO: Stand thee by, Friar. Father, by your leave –
Will you with free and unconstrained soul
Give me this maid your daughter?

26   *counterpoise*, match, weigh equal.

28   *learn*, teach.

29–30   *There ... friend.* Is the movement – courteous, violent, con-
        temptuous? Any movement by Hero?

30–1   *Give ... honour*, i.e. the unblemished outward appearance hides
        the rottenness within.

32   *maid*, virgin. *she blushes*. Normally a sign of modesty. Proverbially
        'red (blushing) is the sign of grace'.

33   *authority*, credibility, guarantee.

35   *modest evidence*, evidence of modesty.

36   *witness*, bear witness to. *simple*, pure.

39   *luxurious*, lecherous, lustful.

41   *mean*, (a) refer to, (b) intend to do.

42   *approved*, confirmed.

43   *your own proof*, yourself in making trial (of her virtue).

46   *known*, had sexual intercourse with.

47–8   *she ... sin.* A contract to marry or simply a declaration before
        witnesses by a man and a woman that they took each other in
        marriage was binding in law. Hence the marriage might be con-
        summated before an actual wedding ceremony. See *Measure for
        Measure*, IV.i.71–2.

48   *extenuate*, lessen (the guilt).

50   *large*, improper, indecent.

54   *write against*, denounce.

55   *Dian ... orb*, the moon, symbol of chastity, in its orbit.

LEONATO: As freely son as God did give her me.

CLAUDIO: And what have I to give you back, whose worth
  May counterpoise this rich and precious gift?

DON PEDRO: Nothing, unless you render her again.

CLAUDIO: Sweet Prince, you learn me noble thankfulness.
  There Leonato, take her back again,
  Give not this rotten orange to your friend –   30
  She's but the sign and semblance of her honour.
  Behold how like a maid she blushes here!
  O what authority and show of truth
  Can cunning sin cover itself withal!
  Comes not that blood as modest evidence
  To witness simple virtue? Would you not swear,
  All you that see her, that she were a maid
  By these exterior shows? But she is none;
  She knows the heat of a luxurious bed.
  Her blush is guiltiness, not modesty.   40

LEONATO: What do you mean, my lord?

CLAUDIO: Not to be married,
  Not to knit my soul to an approved wanton.

LEONATO: Dear my lord, if you in your own proof
  Have vanquished the resistance of her youth,
  And made defeat of her virginity –

CLAUDIO: I know what you would say. If I have known her,
  You will say she did embrace me as a husband,
  And so extenuate the 'forehand sin.
  No Leonato,
  I never tempted her with word too large,   50
  But, as a brother to his sister, showed
  Bashful sincerity and comely love.

HERO: And seemed I ever otherwise to you?

CLAUDIO: Out on thee, seeming! I will write against it.
  You seem to me as Dian in her orb,

56 *blown*, in flower.
57 *blood*, appetite, desire.
58 *Venus*, goddess of sensual love.
58–9 *those ... sensuality*, those spoilt creatures that give reign to wild sensual gratification.
60 *wide*, (a) far from the truth, (b) immoderately.

63 *common stale*, everyman's whore.

72 *kindly*, natural (as of a father).

75 *beset*, (a) assailed, (b) bestowed (in marriage).
76 *What ... this?* It was the duty of parents to see that their children learned the Catechism before confirmation.
77 *To ... name.* The name Hero symbolized the true love of the faithful Hero of legend. Claudio's reply refers to the opening words of the Catechism in the *Book of Common Prayer*: 'What is your name?'

85 *Why ... maiden.* The argument runs as follows: she has not answered the question. They know there was a man because they saw him, therefore she must be lying.

As chaste as is the bud ere it be blown;
But you are more intemperate in your blood
Than Venus, or those pampered animals
That rage in savage sensuality.

HERO: Is my lord well that he doth speak so wide?   60
LEONATO: Sweet Prince, why speak not you?
DON PEDRO: What should I speak?
I stand dishonoured that have gone about
To link my dear friend to a common stale.
LEONATO: Are these things spoken, or do I but dream?
DON JOHN: Sir, they are spoken, and these things are true.
BENEDICK: This looks not like a nuptial.
HERO: True? O God!
CLAUDIO: Leonato, stand I here?
Is this the Prince? Is this the Prince's brother?
Is this face Hero's? Are our eyes our own?
LEONATO: All this is so; but what of this, my lord?   70
CLAUDIO: Let me but move one question to your daughter;
And by that fatherly and kindly power
That you have in her bid her answer truly.
LEONATO: I charge thee do so, as thou art my child.
HERO: O God defend me! How am I beset!
What kind of catechizing call you this?
CLAUDIO: To make you answer truly to your name.
HERO: Is it not Hero? Who can blot that name
With any just reproach?
CLAUDIO: Marry that can Hero.
Hero itself can blot out Hero's virtue.   80
What man was he talked with you yesternight
Out at your window betwixt twelve and one?
Now if you are a maid, answer to this.
HERO: I talked with no man at that hour my lord.
DON PEDRO: Why then are you no maiden. Leonato,
I am sorry you must hear. Upon mine honour,

143

87   *grieved*, aggrieved, wronged.

90   *liberal*, lecherous.

93–7   *Fie ... misgovernment.* Don John rubs salt into the wound with
       pretended disgust; gloating over his success he hypocritically
       commiserates with Hero.
97   *much misgovernment*, outrageous misconduct.

98–   *O ... gracious.* Is Claudio – bitter, vengeful, distraught, despair-
   106 ing, tortured, in tears (ll. 151–2), deeply in love?
99–   *If... heart*, if your inward grace had matched your beautiful out-
   100 ward grace.
101–2 *most ... purity.* The oxymorons mark the peak of agony. See
       Romeo and Juliet, III.ii.73–85, for Juliet's anguish.

103   *gates of love.* The eyes were the chief gates of love.
104   *conjecture*, doubt, suspicion.

107–12 *Hath ... Friar.* Consider appropriate movement, gesture, and
       stage business. Hero faints. Is she – on the ground, taken to a
       couch, or otherwise tended?

110   *spirits*, vital powers. Spirits were regarded as 'subtle and airy sub-
       stances' in the blood. They set in motion all bodily and mental
       faculties.
111–12 *How ... Hero.* Beatrice weeps (ll. 253–4).

    Myself, my brother, and this grieved Count
    Did see her, hear her, at that hour last night
    Talk with a ruffian at her chamber-window;
    Who hath indeed most like a liberal villain,   90
    Confessed the vile encounters they have had
    A thousand times in secret.
DON JOHN: Fie, fie, they are not to be named my lord,
    Not to be spoke of.
    There is not chastity enough in language
    Without offence to utter them. Thus pretty lady,
    I am sorry for thy much misgovernment.
CLAUDIO: O Hero! What a Hero hadst thou been,
    If half thy outward graces had been placed
    About thy thoughts and counsels of thy heart.   100
    But fare thee well, most foul, most fair. Farewell
    Thou pure impiety and impious purity.
    For thee I'll lock up all the gates of love,
    And on my eyelids shall conjecture hang,
    To turn all beauty into thoughts of harm,
    And never shall it more be gracious.
LEONATO: Hath no man's dagger here a point for me?
                          [Hero swoons
BEATRICE: Why how now cousin, wherefore sink you
    down?
DON JOHN: Come let us go. These things, come thus to
    light,
    Smother her spirits up.   110
           [Exeunt Don Pedro, Don John, and Claudio
BENEDICK: How doth the lady?
BEATRICE: Dead I think. Help, uncle.
    Hero! Why Hero! Uncle! Signor Benedick! Friar!
LEONATO: O Fate, take not away thy heavy hand.
    Death is the fairest cover for her shame
    That may be wished for.

120   *printed . . . blood*, proclaimed by her blushes, or, indelibly branding
        her honour.

124   *on . . . reproaches*, following these shames.

126   *Chid . . . frame*, I complained at nature's miserly ordering of things
        in that I had only one child.

130   *issue*, child.
131   *Who . . . infamy*, who tainted with the stigma of base birth.

133   *loins*, i.e. parentage.
134   *mine*, i.e. Hero.

136–7   *That . . . her*, so precious was she to me that I had no care for myself.
137   *why she*? Leonato breaks off in the stress of feeling.

140   *season give*, make wholesome.

142   *attired in wonder*, rapt in amazement.

BEATRICE: How now cousin Hero?
FRIAR: Have comfort lady.
LEONATO: Dost thou look up?
FRIAR: Yea, wherefore should she not?
LEONATO: Wherefore? Why, doth not every earthly thing
  Cry shame upon her? Could she here deny
  The story that is printed in her blood?   120
  Do not live Hero, do not ope thine eyes.
  For did I think thou wouldst not quickly die,
  Thought I thy spirits were stronger than thy shames,
  Myself would on the rearward of reproaches
  Strike at thy life. Grieved I, I had but one?
  Chid I for that at frugal nature's frame?
  O one too much by thee – why had I one?
  Why ever wast thou lovely in my eyes?
  Why had I not with charitable hand
  Took up a beggar's issue at my gates,   130
  Who smirched thus and mired with infamy,
  I might have said 'No part of it is mine;
  This shame derives itself from unknown loins'?
  But mine, and mine I loved, and mine I praised,
  And mine that I was proud on; mine so much
  That I myself was to myself not mine,
  Valuing of her – why she? O she is fallen
  Into a pit of ink, that the wide sea
  Hath drops too few to wash her clean again
  And salt too little which may season give   140
  To her foul tainted flesh.
BENEDICK: Sir, sir, be patient.
  For my part I am so attired in wonder,
  I know not what to say.
BEATRICE: O on my soul my cousin is belied!
BENEDICK: Lady, were you her bedfellow last night?

148   *Confirmed.* Is it?
148–9   *that . . . iron,* i.e. the strong case against Hero is thus made stronger.

155–6   *And . . . lady,* and allowed matters to continue in this way because
         I was watching the lady.
157   *apparitions,* appearances, expressions.

160–2   *in . . . truth.* A reference to the burning of heretics at the stake.
161   *errors.* Error was the word used for misinterpretation of the
         accepted doctrines of religion. Here it is the disbelief of the princes
         in the truth of her chastity.
163   *reading,* study.
164   *experimental seal,* confirmation of experience.
164–5   *warrant . . . book,* support the theme of my book.

168   *biting,* bitter.

171   *she . . . it.* See note to l. 85.

173   *That . . . nakedness.* Is Leonato speaking more truly than he in-
         tended in the light of 'maiden truth' (l. 162)? In emblems 'naked
         truth' was depicted as a nude girl. *proper,* rightful.

177   *warrant,* justify.

BEATRICE: No truly, not, although until last night,
  I have this twelvemonth been her bedfellow.
LEONATO: Confirmed, confirmed. O that is stronger made
  Which was before barred up with ribs of iron.
  Would the two Princes lie? And Claudio lie,   150
  Who loved her so, that speaking of her foulness,
  Washed it with tears? Hence from her, let her die.
FRIAR: Hear me a little;
  For I have only silent been so long,
  And given way unto this course of fortune,
  By noting of the lady. I have marked
  A thousand blushing apparitions
  To start into her face, a thousand innocent shames
  In angel whiteness beat away those blushes;
  And in her eye there hath appeared a fire,   160
  To burn the errors that these Princes hold
  Against her maiden truth. Call me a fool;
  Trust not my reading nor my observations,
  Which with experimental seal doth warrant
  The tenor of my book. Trust not my age,
  My reverence, calling, nor divinity,
  If this sweet lady lie not guiltless here
  Under some biting error.
LEONATO: Friar, it cannot be.
  Thou seest that all the grace that she hath left
  Is that she will not add to her damnation   170
  A sin of perjury; she not denies it.
  Why seek'st thou then to cover with excuse
  That which appears in proper nakedness?
FRIAR: Lady, what man is he you are accused of?
HERO: They know that do accuse me, I know none.
  If I know more of any man alive
  Than that which maiden modesty doth warrant,
  Let all my sins lack mercy. O my father,

180   *unmeet*, improper.

182   *Refuse*, disown.
183   *misprision*, misunderstanding, mistake.
184   *very ... honour*, peak of honour. *bent*, full drawn. Term from archery.
186   *practice*, devising, working.
187   *Whose ... villainies*, whose spirits labour in the shaping of evils. *toil*, (a) work, (b) plot.

190   *hear of it*, receive a challenge.
191   *dried ... mine*, diminished my vigour.
192   *invention*, power to plan.
193   *means*, financial standing.
194   *reft*, bereft, deprived.
195   *awaked ... kind*, roused in such a way.
196   *policy*, activity, shrewdness.

198   *To ... throughly*, to even scores thoroughly with them.

201   *kept in*, hidden.
202   *publish it*, let it be known.
203   *mourning ostentation*, formal show of mourning.

207   *become of*, result from.

209   *remorse*, pity.

211   *travail*, (a) work, (b) labour (child-birth).

Prove you that any man with me conversed
At hours unmeet, or that I yesternight   180
Maintained the change of words with any creature,
Refuse me, hate me, torture me to death.
FRIAR: There is some strange misprision in the princes.
BENEDICK: Two of them have the very bent of honour;
    And if their wisdoms be misled in this,
    The practice of it lives in John the Bastard,
    Whose spirits toil in frame of villainies.
LEONATO: I know not. If they speak but truth of her,
    These hands shall tear her. If they wrong her honour,
    The proudest of them shall well hear of it.   190
    Time hath not yet so dried this blood of mine,
    Nor age so eat up my invention,
    Nor fortune made such havoc of my means,
    Nor my bad life reft me so much of friends,
    But they shall find awaked in such a kind,
    Both strength of limb, and policy of mind,
    Ability in means, and choice of friends
    To quit me of them throughly.
FRIAR: Pause awhile,
    And let my counsel sway you in this case.
    Your daughter here the princes left for dead;   200
    Let her awhile be secretly kept in,
    And publish it that she is dead indeed.
    Maintain a mourning ostentation,
    And on your family's old monument
    Hang mournful epitaphs, and do all rites
    That appertain unto a burial.
LEONATO: What shall become of this? What will this do?
FRIAR: Marry this well carried, shall on her behalf
    Change slander to remorse – that is some good.
    But not for that dream I on this strange course,   210
    But on this travail look for greater birth.

216–20 *That ... ours.* Proverbially 'the worth of a thing is known only when it is lost'.

218　　*rack*, enlarge.

219　　*virtue*, worth.

222–8 *Th' idea ... indeed,* the thought of her as she was in life will gently take shape in the working of his imagination; every beauty of her living person will appear in more exquisite fashion, more animated, delightful, and vital when presented for the contemplation of his soul, than when she was truly alive.

It was believed that the imagination passed its images to the soul (reason) which judged whether they were good or bad. If good, they passed to the will for action. Here the action is mourning.

226　　*moving.* Some also interpret as 'affecting'.

229　　*liver.* Considered to be the seat of love.

232　　*success*, what follows.

233　　*event*, outcome.

234　　*lay ... likelihood,* foretell, guess.

235　　*But ... false,* but if we should not in any other respect hit the mark. *but this,* i.e. the supposition.

237　　*wonder*, state or amazement.

238　　*sort*, turn out.

240　　*reclusive*, cloistered, secluded.

241　　*injuries*, harm.

243　　*inwardness*, intimate feeling.

She dying, as it must be so maintained,
Upon the instant that she was accused,
Shall be lamented, pitied, and excused
Of every hearer. For it so falls out
That what we have we prize not to the worth
Whiles we enjoy it, but being lacked and lost,
Why then we rack the value, then we find
The virtue that possession would not show us
Whiles it was ours. So will it fare with Claudio.   220
When he shall hear she died upon his words,
Th'idea of her life shall sweetly creep
Into his study of imagination,
And every lovely organ of her life
Shall come apparelled in more precious habit,
More moving, delicate, and full of life,
Into the eye and prospect of his soul,
Than when she lived indeed. Then shall he mourn,
If ever love had interest in his liver,
And wish he had not so accused her –   230
No, though he thought his accusation true.
Let this be so, and doubt not but success
Will fashion the event in better shape
Than I can lay it down in likelihood.
But if all aim but this be levelled false,
The supposition of the lady's death
Will quench the wonder of her infamy.
And if it sort not well, you may conceal her,
As best befits her wounded reputation,
In some reclusive and religious life,   240
Out of all eyes, tongues, minds, and injuries.
BENEDICK: Signor Leonato, let the Friar advise you;
  And though you know my inwardness and love
  Is very much unto the Prince and Claudio,
  Yet, by mine honour, I will deal in this

247   *flow*, (a) melt, (b) move easily.

248   *twine*, thread.
       Is Leonato – weak, easily swayed, headstrong, impulsive, harsh,
       melodramatic, comic, outrageous?
249   *Presently*, at once.
250   *to ... cure*. Proverbially 'desperate ills need desperate remedies'.
       The alliteration is 'strangely' strained.
251   *die to live*. The paradox is apt from a friar. (See *II Cor.*, vi.9.)
252   *prolonged*, postponed.
       What is the purpose of the quatrain – to mark the end of a section,
       to stress the aphorisms and counsel of the friar?

259   *right her*, redress her wrongs.

261   *even*, plain. Perhaps a quibble on 'way to get even'.

263   *office*, work.

266–9 *As ... nothing*. Is Beatrice – confused, flustered, taken off guard,
       teasing, emotional, disturbed? She makes much ado about 'noth-
       ing'.

271   *eat it*, (a) the words of the oath, recant, (b) the sword. See *I Henry
       IV*, V.iv.148.

275   *sauce*. Even the sauce of sharp mocking will not make Benedick
       swallow his words. See II.iii.222–8, and *As You Like It*, III.v.68;
       Romeo and Juliet, II.iv.70.

As secretly and justly as your soul
Should with your body.

LEONATO: Being that I flow in grief,
The smallest twine may lead me.

FRIAR: 'Tis well consented. Presently away;
For to strange sores strangely they strain the cure.   250
Come lady, die to live; this wedding-day
Perhaps is but prolonged. Have patience and endure.

[*Exeunt all but Benedick and Beatrice*

BENEDICK: Lady Beatrice, have you wept all this while?

BEATRICE: Yea, and I will weep a while longer.

BENEDICK: I will not desire that.

BEATRICE: You have no reason, I do it freely.

BENEDICK: Surely I do believe your fair cousin is wronged.

BEATRICE: Ah, how much might the man deserve of me
that would right her!

BENEDICK: Is there any way to show such friendship? 260

BEATRICE: A very even way, but no such friend.

BENEDICK: May a man do it?

BEATRICE: It is a man's office, but not yours.

BENEDICK: I do love nothing in the world so well as you.
Is not that strange?

BEATRICE: As strange as the thing I know not. It were as
possible for me to say I loved nothing so well as you. But
believe me not, and yet I lie not; I confess nothing, nor I
deny nothing. I am sorry for my cousin.

BENEDICK: By my sword Beatrice, thou lovest me.   270

BEATRICE: Do not swear, and eat it.

BENEDICK: I will swear by it that you love me; and I will
make him eat it that says I love not you.

BEATRICE: Will you not eat your word?

BENEDICK: With no sauce that can be devised to it. I protest
I love thee.

BEATRICE: Why then God forgive me.

279   *stayed ... hour*, interrupted me at a favourable moment.
280   *protest*, swear.

283   *protest*, object.

285   *Kill Claudio*. On these two words the mood of the scene changes
       from playful tenderness to fierce earnestness. How should they
       be spoken?

289   *I ... here*, in spirit I have gone, though my body remains here.
290   *Nay ... go*. How is Benedick holding her?

297   *approved ... height*, proved to the hilt.

299   *bear ... hand*, lead her with false pretence.
300   *uncovered*, blatant.
301   *unmitigated*, harsh, savage.
302   *eat ... market-place*, tear him to pieces in public.

304   *proper*. Sarcastic.

308   *undone*, ruined.

311   *count*, detail of a charge or accusation. *Comfect*, lollipop.

BENEDICK: What offence sweet Beatrice?

BEATRICE: You have stayed me in a happy hour; I was about to protest I loved you.   280

BENEDICK: And do it with all thy heart.

BEATRICE: I love you with so much of my heart that none is left to protest.

BENEDICK: Come bid me do anything for thee.

BEATRICE: Kill Claudio.

BENEDICK: Ha, not for the wide world.

BEATRICE: You kill me to deny it. Farewell.

BENEDICK: Tarry sweet Beatrice.

BEATRICE: I am gone though I am here. There is no love in you. Nay I pray you, let me go.   290

BENEDICK: Beatrice –

BEATRICE: In faith I will go.

BENEDICK: We'll be friends first.

BEATRICE: You dare easier be friends with me than fight with mine enemy.

BENEDICK: Is Claudio thine enemy?

BEATRICE: Is he not approved in the height a villain that hath slandered, scorned, dishonoured my kinswoman? O that I were a man! What, bear her in hand until they come to take hands, and then with public accusation, uncovered slander, unmitigated rancour – O God that I were a man! I would eat his heart in the market-place.   302

BENEDICK: Hear me Beatrice –

BEATRICE: Talk with a man out at a window – a proper saying!

BENEDICK: Nay but Beatrice –

BEATRICE: Sweet Hero, she is wronged, she is slandered, she is undone.

BENEDICK: Beat–   309

BEATRICE: Princes and counties! Surely a princely testimony, a goodly count, Count Comfect; a sweet gallant

312   *for his sake*, to deal with him.

313–14 *melted into curtsies*. The image of obsequiousness, 'comfect –
       sweet – melted – curtsies' is often used by Shakespeare.

314–15 *men ... tongue*, men are now only pretty speech makers.

315   *trim*, fine, slick (ironic).

315–16 *He ... it*, i.e. words not deeds now establish a reputation for
       valour.
       Do you agree with Beatrice's attack on Claudio and Don Pedro?

320–1 *Use ... it*, i.e. by fighting a duel.

325   *I am engaged*, I'll take it on.

327   *render ... account*, (a) pay dearly, (b) pay bitterly (dire).

       Another deftly constructed scene. Claudio's calumniation of Hero
       at the beginning is balanced by Beatrice's condemnation of Clau-
       dio at the end, pivoted by the Friar's faith and practical counsel.
       Similarly a love lost is matched by a love gained. The shock of
       Claudio's rejection of Hero makes a continuance of the 'merry
       war' between Benedick and Beatrice impossible. Their con-
       fessions of love are made with grave tenderness, just a slight with-
       holding by Beatrice and a gentle wry quibble. Immediately their
       love is forged by Beatrice's demand, 'Kill Claudio'.

A prison

S.D.   Q 'Enter the Constables, Borachio, and the Towne clearke in
       gownes'. The Town Clerk, i.e. parish clerk, is called the Sexton
       in the speech-headings.
       gowns. A black gown was the dress on formal occasions of a con-
       stable and of a sexton.
       Some properties will be required – seats, benches, inkhorn, quill
       pen, paper, cushion, stool.

1   *dissembly*. A perversion of 'assembly'. As such the word suggests
       a 'disorderly assembly'. If it is based on 'dissemble', it could be
       taken to mean 'that which one pretends not to see', which gives
       it an interesting relationship with 'appeared'. *appeared*, (a) in view,
       (b) put in an attendance at court.

surely! O that I were a man for his sake, or that I had any friend would be man for my sake! But manhood is melted into curtsies, valour into compliment, and men are only turned into tongue, and trim ones too. He is now as valiant as Hercules that only tells a lie and swears it. I cannot be a man with wishing, therefore I will die a woman with grieving.

BENEDICK: Tarry good Beatrice. By this hand I love thee.

BEATRICE: Use it for my love some other way than swearing by it.   321

BENEDICK: Think you in your soul the Count Claudio hath wronged Hero?

BEATRICE: Yea, as sure as I have a thought or a soul.

BENEDICK: Enough, I am engaged; I will challenge him. I will kiss your hand, and so I leave you. By this hand, Claudio shall render me a dear account. As you hear of me, so think of me. Go comfort your cousin. I must say she is dead – and so farewell.   [*Exeunt*

SCENE TWO

Enter DOGBERRY, VERGES, *and the* SEXTON *in gowns;*
and the WATCH, *with* CONRADE *and* BORACHIO

DOGBERRY: Is our whole dissembly appeared?

VERGES: O a stool and a cushion for the Sexton.

SEXTON: Which be the malefactors?

DOGBERRY: Marry that am I and my partner.

5   *exhibition*, commission, authority. But Dogberry may be confused with 'exhibit', document or object submitted for examination in a court of law.

12   *sirrah*. A term of contempt.

13   *I ... sir*. Conrade bristles at being called 'sirrah'.

18   *defend*, forbid.

19–21 *it ... shortly*. Dogberry has transposed 'proved' and 'thought so'.

20   *go ... be*, is likely to be.

23   *witty*, clever, cunning.

24   *go about with*, deal with, outwit, set about.

28–9 *both ... tale*, both agree in their story. Dogberry suspects collusion!

32   *eftest*, readiest.

VERGES: Nay that's certain. We have the exhibition to examine.

SEXTON: But which are the offenders that are to be examined? Let them come before Master Constable.

DOGBERRY: Yea marry, let them come before me. What is your name, friend? 10

BORACHIO: Borachio.

DOGBERRY: Pray write down, Borachio. Yours sirrah?

CONRADE: I am a gentleman sir, and my name is Conrade.

DOGBERRY: Write down Master Gentleman Conrade. Masters, do you serve God?

CONRADE *and* BORACHIO: Yes sir we hope.

DOGBERRY: Write down, that they hope they serve God. And write God first, for God defend but God should go before such villains. Masters, it is proved already that you are little better than false knaves, and it will go near to be thought so shortly. How answer you for yourselves? 21

CONRADE: Marry sir we say we are none.

DOGBERRY: A marvellous witty fellow, I assure you; but I will go about with him. Come you hither sirrah; a word in your ear. Sir, I say to you, it is thought you are false knaves.

BORACHIO: Sir, I say to you we are none.

DOGBERRY: Well, stand aside. 'Fore God they are both in a tale. Have you writ down that they are none?

SEXTON: Master Constable, you go not the way to examine. You must call forth the watch that are their accusers. 31

DOGBERRY: Yea marry, that's the eftest way. Let the watch come forth. Masters, I charge you in the Prince's name accuse these men.

FIRST WATCHMAN: This man said sir, that Don John the Prince's brother was a villain.

38   *flat*, outright. *perjury*, uttering false evidence while on oath. Dogberry argues that the brother of the Prince cannot be a villain
(base-born), therefore Borachio is lying, and that, he believes, is
perjury. Ironically Don John has confessed that he is a 'plain-
dealing villain' (I.iii.29).

46   *burglary*, i.e. ? bribery.

50   *upon his words*, as the result of his testimony.

53   *redemption*, i.e. perdition.

62   *opinioned*, pinioned.

64   *coxcomb*, conceited fool.
65   *God's my life*, God save my life.

67   *naughty*, wicked. *varlet*, wretch.

69   *suspect*, i.e. respect.

DOGBERRY: Write down 'Prince John a villain'. Why this is flat perjury, to call a prince's brother villain.

BORACHIO: Master Constable –

DOGBERRY: Pray thee, fellow, peace. I do not like thy look I promise thee.   41

SEXTON: What heard you him say else?

SECOND WATCHMAN: Marry that he had received a thousand ducats of Don John for accusing the Lady Hero wrongfully.

DOGBERRY: Flat burglary as ever was committed.

VERGES: Yea by mass that it is.

SEXTON: What else fellow?

FIRST WATCHMAN: And that Count Claudio did mean, upon his words, to disgrace Hero before the whole assembly, and not marry her.   51

DOGBERRY: O villain! Thou wilt be condemned into everlasting redemption for this.

SEXTON: What else?

SECOND WATCHMAN: This is all.

SEXTON: And this is more, masters, than you can deny. Prince John is this morning secretly stolen away. Hero was in this manner accused, in this very manner refused, and upon the grief of this suddenly died. Master Constable, let these men be bound, and brought to Leonato's. I will go before and show him their examination.   [*Exit*

DOGBERRY: Come let them be opinioned.   62

VERGES: Let them be – in the hands.

CONRADE: Off coxcomb!

DOGBERRY: God's my life, where's the Sexton? Let him write down the Prince's officer coxcomb. Come, bind them. Thou naughty varlet!

CONRADE: Away, you are an ass, you are an ass.   68

DOGBERRY: Dost thou not suspect my place? Dost thou not suspect my years? O that he were here to write me

73   *piety*, i.e. ? iniquity, impiety.

76   *pretty ... flesh*, i.e. handsome.
77–9 *rich ... gowns*, i.e. one who is well enough off. See III.v.25.

Shakespeare slips in the essential point of the scene quickly and unobtrusively, concentrating attention on Dogberry's malad-ministration of his function and of the English language – why?

down an ass! But masters, remember that I am an ass; though it be not written down, yet forget not that I am an ass. No thou villain, thou art full of piety, as shall be proved upon thee by good witness. I am a wise fellow, and which is more, an officer; and which is more, a house-holder; and which is more, as pretty a piece of flesh as any is in Messina; and one that knows the law, go to; and a rich fellow enough, go to; and a fellow that hath had losses; and one that hath two gowns and everything handsome about him. Bring him away. O that I had been writ down an ass!   [*Exeunt*

2-3   *And ... yourself.* A variation on the proverb, 'To lament the dead avails not and to the living it is hurtful'.

2   *second*, support.

7   *suit with*, match.

12   *answer*, (a) correspond, (b) respond in antiphon. *strain*, (a) injury, (b) trait, (c) tune.

15   *stroke his beard*, appear wise, reflect.

16   *sorrow wag.* Q, F 'sorrow, wagge'. Much disputed. Most editors print 'sorry wag', pitiful jester. Others read 'sorrow wag', drive away sorrow. A simple reading is 'sorrowing', and the line rendered, 'And when sorrowing, merely cry "hem" instead of groaning'. *cry 'hem!* ', merely clear his throat.

17   *Patch*, mend. *proverbs.* See I.i.254–6, *Coriolanus*, I.i.208–11, and *Henry V*, II.ii.115–17 for the inadequacy of proverbs to support an argument.

17-18   *make ... candle-wasters*, bemuse sorrow with philosophy.

18   *candle-wasters*, book-worms, students.

20-31   *men ... himself.* Variations on two proverbs: 'It is easy for a sound man to give counsel to the sick', and, 'All commend patience, but none can endure to suffer'.

ACT FIVE

SCENE ONE

Enter LEONATO *and his brother* ANTONIO

ANTONIO: If you go on thus, you will kill yourself,
  And 'tis not wisdom thus to second grief
  Against yourself.
LEONATO: I pray thee cease thy counsel,
  Which falls into mine ears as profitless
  As water in a sieve. Give not me counsel,
  Nor let no comforter delight mine ear,
  But such a one whose wrongs do suit with mine.
  Bring me a father that so loved his child,
  Whose joy of her is overwhelmed like mine,
  And bid him speak of patience;   10
  Measure his woe the length and breadth of mine,
  And let it answer every strain for strain,
  And thus for thus, and such a grief for such,
  In every lineament, branch, shape, and form.
  If such a one will smile and stroke his beard,
  And sorrow wag, cry 'hem!' when he should groan,
  Patch grief with proverbs, make misfortune drunk
  With candle-wasters – bring him yet to me,
  And I of him will gather patience.
  But there is no such man; for brother, men   20
  Can counsel and speak comfort to that grief
  Which they themselves not feel; but tasting it,

23   *passion*, grief, agony. *which*, who.
24   *preceptial medicine*, remedy of moral rules. *rage*, madness, anguish.

26   *Charm*, remove pain. *air*, i.e. breath of magic words.
27   *office*, business.
28   *wring*, are tortured, writhe.
29   *virtue*, power, integrity. *sufficiency*, ability, capacity.

32   *advertisement*, advice.

37–8 *However . . . sufferance*, although they have written as if they were all-knowing as gods and scorned misfortune and vicissitude.
38   *push*, mock, scorn.
39–40 *Yet . . . too*. Proverbially 'to lament the dead avails not, and revenge vents hatred'.
39   *bend*, direct, turn.

49   *hasty now*. Sarcastic. *all is one*, never mind.
50   *Nay . . . man*. Any action required?

Their counsel turns to passion, which before
Would give preceptial medicine to rage,
Fetter strong madness in a silken thread,
Charm ache with air, and agony with words.
No, no; 'tis all men's office to speak patience
To those that wring under the load of sorrow,
But no man's virtue nor sufficiency
To be so moral when he shall endure   30
The like himself. Therefore give me no counsel,
My griefs cry louder than advertisement.

ANTONIO: Therein do men from children nothing differ.

LEONATO: I pray thee peace. I will be flesh and blood;
For there was never yet philosopher
That could endure the toothache patiently,
However they have writ the style of gods,
And made a push at chance and sufferance.

ANTONIO: Yet bend not all the harm upon yourself;
Make those that do offend you suffer too.   40

LEONATO: There thou speak'st reason. Nay I will do so.
My soul doth tell me Hero is belied,
And that shall Claudio know; so shall the Prince,
And all of them that thus dishonour her.

ANTONIO: Here comes the Prince and Claudio hastily.

Enter DON PEDRO *and* CLAUDIO

DON PEDRO: Good-e'en, good-e'en.

CLAUDIO: Good day to both of you.

LEONATO: Hear you my lords—

DON PEDRO: We have some haste Leonato.

LEONATO: Some haste my lord! Well, fare you well my
   lord.
   Are you so hasty now? Well, all is one.   49

DON PEDRO: Nay, do not quarrel with us, good old man.

53   *dissembler*, deceiver.

54   *Nay ... sword.* Claudio's instinctive reaction which he imme-
      diately regrets.
55   *beshrew*, curse.

58   *fleer*, mock.
59   *dotard*, old dodderer.

62   *head*, face.

64   *reverence*, dignity.
65   *bruise ... days*, battering of time. Compare *Romeo and Juliet*,
      II.iii.37, 'unbruised youth'.
66   *trial ... man*, duel.

71   *framed*, devised.

75   *nice fence*, elegant fencing. A glance at the slender rapier in favour
      with young men in contrast with the old-fashioned sword with
      a cutting edge.
76   *May ... lustihood*, prime of youth and full flower of his vigour.
78   *daff me*, push me off. Any movement or gesture?

ANTONIO: If he could right himself with quarrelling,
  Some of us would lie low.
CLAUDIO: Who wrongs him?
LEONATO: Marry thou dost wrong me, thou dissembler,
      thou.
  Nay, never lay thy hand upon thy sword;
  I fear thee not.
CLAUDIO: Marry beshrew my hand,
  If it should give your age such cause of fear.
  In faith my hand meant nothing to my sword.
LEONATO: Tush, tush man, never fleer and jest at me.
  I speak not like a dotard nor a fool,
  As under privilege of age to brag   60
  What I have done being young, or what would do
  Were I not old. Know, Claudio, to thy head,
  Thou hast so wronged mine innocent child and me
  That I am forced to lay my reverence by,
  And with grey hairs and bruise of many days,
  Do challenge thee to trial of a man.
  I say thou hast belied mine innocent child.
  Thy slander hath gone through and through her heart,
  And she lies buried with her ancestors –
  O, in a tomb where never scandal slept,   70
  Save this of hers, framed by thy villainy!
CLAUDIO: My villainy?
LEONATO: Thine Claudio, thine I say.
DON PEDRO: You say not right old man.
LEONATO: My lord, my lord,
  I'll prove it on his body if he dare,
  Despite his nice fence and his active practice,
  His May of youth and bloom of lustihood.
CLAUDIO: Away, I will not have to do with you.
LEONATO: Canst thou so daff me? Thou hast killed my
      child;

80– *He ... this.* What is the reason for Antonio's sudden change from
101 counselling patience to extravagant aggressiveness – the attitude
     of Claudio and Don Pedro, quarrelsomeness, desire to support
     his brother, to enlarge the quarrel and thus ensure the fight?
82   *Win ... me*, let him beat me before boasting about it. Proverbial.
84   *foining*, thrusting.

90   *serpent ... tongue.* The serpent's tongue was believed to be a
     poisonous sting.
91   *apes*, fools. *Jacks*, knaves.

93   *they weigh*, they are worth. *utmost scruple*, least amount. *scruple*.
     A very small weight of twenty grains apothecary's measure.
94   *Scrambling*, disorderly, scuffling. *out-facing*, insolent. *fashion-*
     monging, fashion changing.
95   *cog*, cheat. *flout*, jeer. *deprave*, speak ill of, defame.
96   *anticly*, grotesquely, like buffoons. *show outward hideousness*, put
     on a frightening appearance.
97   *dangerous*, threatening, arrogant.
     Is Antonio – quarrelsome, foolish, comical, ludicrous, undigni-
     fied, serious, assuming the 'sword of Justice'?

102 *wake*, disturb your patience. See *Richard II*, I.iii.132, 'wake our
     peace', i.e. disturb our peace. Don Pedro is ironic. See ll. 112–
     13.

If thou kill'st me, boy, thou shalt kill a man.

ANTONIO: He shall kill two of us, and men indeed   80
   But that's no matter, let him kill one first.
   Win me and wear me; let him answer me.
   Come follow me boy; come sir boy, come follow me.
   Sir boy, I'll whip you from your foining fence.
   Nay, as I am a gentleman, I will.

LEONATO: Brother –

ANTONIO: Content yourself. God knows I loved my niece,
   And she is dead, slandered to death by villains,
   That dare as well answer a man indeed
   As I dare take a serpent by the tongue.   90
   Boys, apes, braggarts, Jacks, milksops!

LEONATO: Brother Antony –

ANTONIO: Hold you content. What, man! I know them,
    yea,
   And what they weigh, even to the utmost scruple –
   Scrambling, out-facing, fashion-monging boys,
   That lie and cog and flout, deprave, and slander,
   Go anticly, show outward hideousness,
   And speak off half a dozen dangerous words,
   How they might hurt their enemies, if they durst,
   And this is all.

LEONATO: But brother Antony –

ANTONIO: Come 'tis no matter. 100
   Do not you meddle, let me deal in this.

DON PEDRO: Gentlemen both, we will not wake your
    patience.
   My heart is sorry for your daughter's death,
   But on my honour she was charged with nothing
   But what was true and very full of proof.

LEONATO: My lord, my lord –

DON PEDRO: I will not hear you.

LEONATO: No?

110   Why the change to prose?

112–13 *almost, almost.* Don Pedro continues his irony.

117   *doubt,* suspect, fear.

122   *high-proof melancholy,* in a stubborn melancholy. *fain,* gladly.

127   *beside their wit,* mad. *draw,* i.e. (a) musical instrument from its case, (b) his sword of wit.

131–2 *care . . . cat.* Proverbial.
132   *mettle,* spirit, courage.
133   *in the career,* head-on, in a charge. The image is from tourneying in the tilt-yard. *an,* if.
134   *charge,* level (as a spear in a tournament).
135   *staff,* spear.
136   *broke cross,* broken in the middle through not hitting truly. A sign of clumsiness or a mark of dishonour in tilting.

Come brother, away. I will be heard.

ANTONIO: And shall, or some of us will smart for it.

[Exeunt Leonato and Antonio

DON PEDRO: See see, here comes the man we went to seek.

Enter BENEDICK

CLAUDIO: Now signor, what news?   110

BENEDICK: Good day my lord.

DON PEDRO: Welcome signor, you are almost come to part almost a fray.

CLAUDIO: We had like to have had our two noses snapped off with two old men without teeth.

DON PEDRO: Leonato and his brother. What think'st thou? Had we fought, I doubt we should have been too young for them.

BENEDICK: In a false quarrel there is no true valour. I came to seek you both.   120

CLAUDIO: We have been up and down to seek thee, for we are high-proof melancholy, and would fain have it beaten away. Wilt thou use thy wit?

BENEDICK: It is in my scabbard – shall I draw it?

DON PEDRO: Dost thou wear thy wit by thy side?

CLAUDIO: Never any did so, though very many have been beside their wit. I will bid thee draw, as we do the minstrels – draw to pleasure us.

DON PEDRO: As I am an honest man he looks pale. Art thou sick, or angry?   130

CLAUDIO: What, courage, man! What though care killed a cat, thou hast mettle enough in thee to kill care.

BENEDICK: Sir, I shall meet your wit in the career, an you charge it against me. I pray you choose another subject.

CLAUDIO: Nay then, give him another staff – this last was broke cross.

137   *changes*, i.e. his facial expression.
139   *to ... girdle*, to put up with it. Proverbially 'if you be angry you
       may turn the buckle of your girdle behind you'. Said to one angry
       over a small matter whose anger is as little valued.

143   *make it good*, prove it by deeds.
144   *Do me right*, give me satisfaction, i.e. accept my challenge. *protest*,
       proclaim.

147   *meet*, (a) satisfy, (b) fight. *good cheer*, (a) cheerfulness, i.e. lose his
       melancholy, (b) good food.
149–50 *calf's head*, fool, clown.
150   *capon*, castrated cockerel, feeble creature. *carve most curiously*, cut
       him up skilfully, pink him precisely.
151   *woodcock*, simpleton, nit-wit.
152   *ambles*, goes sluggishly, at an easy pace.

154,155 *fine*, (a) excellent, (b) small.
155   *great*, profound.
156   *great gross*, large crude.

158   *wise gentleman*. Ironic. Perhaps = 'wiseacre'.
159   *hath the tongues*, is an accomplished linguist.

161   *double tongue*, deceiver.
162   *trans-shape*, change round, distort.

164   *properest*, handsomest.

167–8 *an ... dearly*. Proverbially 'a woman either loves or hates to
       extremes'.

DON PEDRO: By this light he changes more and more. I think he be angry indeed.

CLAUDIO: If he be, he knows how to turn his girdle.

BENEDICK: Shall I speak a word in your ear? 140

CLAUDIO: God bless me from a challenge!

BENEDICK: [*Aside to Claudio*] You are a villain – I jest not. I will make it good how you dare, with what you dare, and when you dare. Do me right, or I will protest your cowardice. You have killed a sweet lady, and her death shall fall heavy on you. Let me hear from you.

CLAUDIO: Well I will meet you, so I may have good cheer.

DON PEDRO: What, a feast, a feast?

CLAUDIO: I'faith I thank him. He hath bid me to a calf's head and a capon, the which if I do not carve most curiously, say my knife's naught. Shall I not find a woodcock too?

BENEDICK: Sir your wit ambles well, it goes easily. 152

DON PEDRO: I'll tell thee how Beatrice praised thy wit the other day. I said thou hadst a fine wit. 'True,' said she, 'a fine little one.' 'No,' said I, 'a great wit.' 'Right,' says she, 'a great gross one.' 'Nay,' said I, 'a good wit.' 'Just,' said she, 'it hurts nobody.' 'Nay,' said I, 'the gentleman is wise.' 'Certain,' said she, 'a wise gentleman.' 'Nay,' said I, 'he hath the tongues.' 'That I believe,' said she, 'for he swore a thing to me on Monday night, which he forswore on Tuesday morning. There's a double tongue, there's two tongues.' Thus did she an hour together trans-shape thy particular virtues; yet at last she concluded with a sigh, thou wast the properest man in Italy. 164

CLAUDIO: For the which she wept heartily and said she cared not.

DON PEDRO: Yea that she did; but yet, for all that, an if she did not hate him deadly, she would love him dearly. The old man's daughter told us all.

170–1 *God ... garden.* See *Gen.*, iii.8–10. A reference back to Benedick in the arbour (II.iii). Perhaps, too, a parallel with the fact that in Eden Adam had eaten of the tree of knowledge and his eyes were opened.

172–5 *set ... man.* See I.i.233–8. Don Pedro echoes Benedick's own words. Benedick fails to see the point of the mockery.

177 *gossip-like humour,* mood for chattering about personalities.

177–9 *break ... not,* i.e. boasters break swords but not in fights. So Falstaff hacked his sword (*I Henry IV,* II.iv.275–7).

187 *for ... Beatrice.* An ironic reward for their contriving.

190–1 *What ... wit,* what a stupid creature a man is for all his manly doublet and hose when he has laid aside his wit like his cloak.

190 *pretty,* fine. Ironic.

192–3 *He ... man,* he then appears a great fellow to a fool, though in reality a fool is a wise man by comparison.

194 *soft you,* be quiet.

194–5 *Pluck ... sad,* let me pull myself together and be serious.

194 *Pluck up,* let me rouse. *heart,* spirits.

S.D. Should the Watch's entry be an attempt at formality, or timorous, or with panache led by Dogberry at his most pompous?

197 *reasons,* (a) evidence, (b) raisins.

198 *cursing,* cursed. See *Matt.,* xxiii.13, 29. 'Woe unto you Scribes and Pharisees hypocrites'.

CLAUDIO: All, all, and moreover, God saw him when he
was hid in the garden.   171

DON PEDRO: But when shall we set the savage bull's horns
on the sensible Benedick's head?

CLAUDIO: Yea, and text underneath, 'Here dwells Benedick
the married man'?

BENEDICK: Fare you well boy, you know my mind. I will
leave you now to your gossip-like humour. You break
jests as braggarts do their blades, which, God be thanked,
hurt not. [*To Don Pedro*] My lord, for your many courtesies
I thank you. I must discontinue your company. Your
brother the Bastard is fled from Messina. You have among
you killed a sweet and innocent lady. For my Lord Lackbeard there, he and I shall meet, and till then peace be with
him.   [*Exit*

DON PEDRO: He is in earnest.   185

CLAUDIO: In most profound earnest, and I'll warrant you,
for the love of Beatrice.

DON PEDRO: And hath challenged thee.

CLAUDIO: Most sincerely.

DON PEDRO: What a pretty thing man is when he goes in
his doublet and hose and leaves off his wit.   191

CLAUDIO: He is then a giant to an ape, but then is an ape a
doctor to such a man.

DON PEDRO: But soft you, let me be. Pluck up my heart,
and be sad. Did he not say my brother was fled?

Enter DOGBERRY, VERGES, WATCH, CONRADE,
and BORACHIO

DOGBERRY: Come you sir, if justice cannot tame you, she
shall ne'er weigh more reasons in her balance. Nay, an you
be a cursing hypocrite once, you must be looked to.

DON PEDRO: How now, two of my brother's men bound?
Borachio one!   200

201 *Hearken after*, inquire into.

203–7 *Marry ... knaves.* Dogberry in effect repeats the charge. How much of this ironically applies to Claudio and Don Pedro?
205 *slanders*, slanderers.

212 *Rightly ... division*, correctly stated each placed in its correct logical section.
213 *one ... suited*, one meaning aptly expressed (in four ways). *suited*, clothed (with words).
215 *bound ... answer*, prisoners to answer charges.
216 *cunning*, clever, learned.

220 *shallow*, small brained.

222 *incensed me*, set me on.
From l. 110 Don Pedro and Claudio have been conversing lightheartedly in prose. Now after Borachio's confession the depth of their emotion is expressed in verse.

230 *Runs ... blood.* Perhaps an echo of 'the iron entered into his soul', *Psalm cv.*18 (*Great Bible*).

CLAUDIO: Hearken after their offence my lord.

DON PEDRO: Officers, what offence have these men done?

DOGBERRY: Marry sir, they have committed false report; moreover they have spoken untruths; secondarily, they are slanders; sixth and lastly, they have belied a lady; thirdly, they have verified unjust things; and to conclude, they are lying knaves.

DON PEDRO: First I ask thee what they have done; thirdly I ask thee what's their offence; sixth and lastly why they are committed; and to conclude, what you lay to their charge. 211

CLAUDIO: Rightly reasoned, and in his own division, and, by my troth, there's one meaning well suited.

DON PEDRO: Who have you offended masters, that you are thus bound to your answer? This learned Constable is too cunning to be understood. What's your offence?

BORACHIO: Sweet Prince, let me go no farther to mine answer. Do you hear me, and let this Count kill me. I have deceived even your very eyes. What your wisdoms could not discover, these shallow fools have brought to light, who in the night overheard me confessing to this man how Don John your brother incensed me to slander the Lady Hero, how you were brought into the orchard and saw me court Margaret in Hero's garments, how you disgraced her when you should marry her. My villainy they have upon record, which I had rather seal with my death than repeat over to my shame. The lady is dead upon mine and my master's false accusation; and briefly, I desire nothing but the reward of a villain.

DON PEDRO: Runs not this speech like iron through your blood? 230

CLAUDIO: I have drunk poison whiles he uttered it.

DON PEDRO: But did my brother set thee on to this?

BORACHIO: Yea, and paid me richly for the practice of it.

236–7   *Sweet ... first.* Claudio's love is restored not upon news of her death (IV.i.220–8) but of her innocence.
237   *rare semblance*, exquisite likeness.
238   *plaintiffs*, i.e. defendants.
239   *reformed*, i.e. informed.
240–1   *masters ... ass.* Is this an implicit ironic comment on the wisdom of Don Pedro and Claudio?

244–6   *Let ... him.* The eyes were considered to be the index of the mind, betraying both the evil and the good in a man's character.

248   *breath*, words, story.

251   *honourable.* Sarcastic. Should the audience be amused at the dramatic irony that the tables are turned on Don Pedro and Claudio. Should Leonato betray any signs of enjoyment of his position?

258   *Impose me to*, inflict on me.

259–60 *yet ... mistaking.* Is this all?

262   *bend under*, submit to.

DON PEDRO : He is composed and framed of treachery,
And fled he is upon this villainy.

CLAUDIO : Sweet Hero, now thy image doth appear
In the rare semblance that I loved it first.

DOGBERRY : Come, bring away the plaintiffs. By this time
our Sexton hath reformed Signor Leonato of the matter.
And masters, do not forget to specify when time and place
shall serve, that I am an ass.   241

VERGES : Here, here come master Signor Leonato, and the
Sexton too.

Enter LEONATO *and* ANTONIO, *with the* SEXTON

LEONATO : Which is the villain? Let me see his eyes,
That, when I note another man like him,
I may avoid him. Which of these is he?

BORACHIO : If you would know your wronger, look on me.

LEONATO : Art thou the slave that with thy breath hast killed
Mine innocent child?

BORACHIO :   Yea, even I alone.

LEONATO : No, not so villain, thou beliest thyself.   250
Here stand a pair of honourable men,
A third is fled, that had a hand in it.
I thank you Princes for my daughter's death,
Record it with your high and worthy deeds.
'Twas bravely done, if you bethink you of it.

CLAUDIO : I know not how to pray your patience,
Yet I must speak. Choose your revenge yourself;
Impose me to what penance your invention
Can lay upon my sin – yet sinned I not
But in mistaking.

DON PEDRO :   By my soul not I,   260
And yet to satisfy this good old man,
I would bend under any heavy weight
That he'll enjoin me to.

266 *Possess*, inform.

268 *labour ... invention*, compose anything inspired by sorrow.
269 *Hang ... tomb*. A contemporary custom. See IV.i.203–6. *epitaph*, memorial verse.

275 *she ... both*. But see I.ii.2. Antonio has a son. The point is that she is adequately dowered.

278–80 *Your ... Claudio*. Is Claudio unduly tearful? See IV.i.150–2.

282 *naughty*, wicked.

284 *packed*, involved.

286 *Nor, not*. The double negative is emphatic.

289–90 *under ... black*, confirmed in writing.

292 *one Deformed*. See III.iii.120–2.

LEONATO: I cannot bid you bid my daughter live –
  That were impossible – but I pray you both,
  Possess the people in Messina here
  How innocent she died; and if your love
  Can labour aught in sad invention,
  Hang her an epitaph upon her tomb,
  And sing it to her bones, sing it tonight.   270
  Tomorrow morning come you to my house;
  And since you could not be my son-in-law,
  Be yet my nephew. My brother hath a daughter,
  Almost the copy of my child that's dead,
  And she alone is heir to both of us.
  Give her the right you should have given her cousin,
  And so dies my revenge.
CLAUDIO: O noble sir!
  Your over-kindness doth wring tears from me.
  I do embrace your offer, and dispose
  For henceforth of poor Claudio.   280
LEONATO: Tomorrow then I will expect your coming;
  Tonight I take my leave. This naughty man
  Shall face to face be brought to Margaret,
  Who I believe was packed in all this wrong,
  Hired to it by your brother.
BORACHIO: No by my soul she was not,
  Nor knew not what she did when she spoke to me,
  But always hath been just and virtuous
  In anything that I do know by her.   288
DOGBERRY: Moreover sir, which indeed is not under white
  and black, this plaintiff here, the offender, did call me ass.
  I beseech you let it be remembered in his punishment. And
  also the watch heard them talk of one Deformed; they say
  he wears a key in his ear and a lock hanging by it, and
  borrows money in God's name, the which he hath used
  so long and never paid, that now men grow hard-hearted

302   *God . . . foundation.* The customary blessing uttered by those who
received alms at the gates of religious foundations. Is this how
Dogberry afforded his 'two gowns'?

315   *lewd*, base, wicked.

Is Claudio – poor, victimized, noble, pliable, easy-going, dignified, outrageous, callous, agonized, tormented, defensive, self-
pitying?

and will lend nothing for God's sake. Pray you examine
him upon that point.

LEONATO: I thank thee for thy care and honest pains.

DOGBERRY: Your worship speaks like a most thankful and
reverend youth, and I praise God for you.   300

LEONATO: There's for thy pains.

DOGBERRY: God save the foundation!

LEONATO: Go, I discharge thee of thy prisoner, and I thank
thee.

DOGBERRY: I leave an arrant knave with your worship,
which I beseech your worship to correct yourself, for the
example of others. God keep your worship, I wish your
worship well, God restore you to health. I humbly give
you leave to depart, and if a merry meeting may be
wished, God prohibit it. Come neighbour.   310
                                    [*Exeunt Dogberry and Verges*

LEONATO: Until tomorrow morning, lords, farewell.

ANTONIO: Farewell my lords, we look for you tomorrow.

DON PEDRO: We will not fail.

CLAUDIO: Tonight I'll mourn with Hero.
                                    [*Exeunt Don Pedro and Claudio*

LEONATO: [*To the Watch*] Bring you these fellows on. We'll
talk with Margaret,

How her acquaintance grew with this lewd fellow.
                                    [*Exeunt*

Much Ado About Nothing

Leonato's orchard

S.D.   How can the entries suggest Benedick's earnestness and Margaret's pert control of the situation?

3   *sonnet.* A verse usually of fourteen lines often addressed by a lover to his lady.

5   *style*, (a) fashion, (b) stile.
6   *come over*, (a) excel, (b) stride over. *comely*. A glance at Margaret's comeliness.

8   *come over*, (a) marry, (b) lie on.
9   *below stairs*, as a servant not a mistress in both senses.

12–13 *blunt ... not*, i.e. blunted practice foils.

15–16 *I ... bucklers*, I give you best. A buckler is a small shield.

19–20 *put ... vice*. The pike was a detachable spike which was screwed into the centre of the buckler.
20   *vice*, screw.
    This exchange of wit has sexual innuendos.

25–8 *The ... deserve*. A song then well known, but no longer extant

29   *Leander*. In Greek story Leander swam across the Hellespont each night to visit his love, Hero of Sestos. He was drowned in a storm and Hero in grief drowned herself.

188

SCENE TWO

Enter BENEDICK *and* MARGARET

BENEDICK: Pray thee sweet Mistress Margaret, deserve well
at my hands by helping me to the speech of Beatrice.

MARGARET: Will you then write me a sonnet in praise of
my beauty?

BENEDICK: In so high a style Margaret, that no man living
shall come over it, for in most comely truth, thou deservest
it.

MARGARET: To have no man come over me? Why, shall I
always keep below stairs?

BENEDICK: Thy wit is as quick as the greyhound's mouth,
it catches.   11

MARGARET: And yours as blunt as the fencer's foils, which
hit, but hurt not.

BENEDICK: A most manly wit Margaret, it will not hurt a
woman. And so I pray thee call Beatrice. I give thee the
bucklers.

MARGARET: Give us the swords, we have bucklers of our
own.

BENEDICK: If you use them Margaret, you must put in the
pikes with a vice; and they are dangerous weapons for
maids.   21

MARGARET: Well, I will call Beatrice to you, who I think
hath legs.   [*Exit Margaret*

BENEDICK: And therefore will come.

  [*Sings*]   The God of love,
               That sits above,
               And knows me, and knows me,
               How pitiful I deserve –   28

  I mean in singing. But in loving – Leander the good

30   *Troilus*. In medieval versions of the siege of Troy, Troilus, the son of king Priam, loved Cressida. Her uncle, Pandarus, arranged for them to consummate their love. Cressida, sent to the Greeks in exchange for her father who had been captured, became Diomed's mistress.

        Both Troilus and Leander were regarded as examples of faithful lovers.

        panders, bawds. Go-betweens who supply whores with customers. The word is derived from Pandarus.

31   *quondam carpet-mongers*, former ladies' men.

36   *innocent*, (a) harmless, silly, (b) of a baby.

37   *babbling*, foolish, childish.

38   *was ... planet*, have no natural gift of writing poetry. See II.i.303.

39   *festival*, joyful, celebratory.

        Is Benedick's failure to compose poetry a demonstration of his sincerity in love, and that he is not the fashionable romantic lover, or a joke at his expense?

48–9   *Foul ... noisome*. Proverbially 'words are but wind'.

54   *subscribe him*, write him down, confirm him as.

58   *politic a state*, well-governed condition.

swimmer, Troilus the first employer of panders, and a whole bookful of these quondam carpet-mongers, whose names yet run smoothly in the even road of a blank verse – why they were never so truly turned over and over as my poor self in love. Marry I cannot show it in rhyme – I have tried. I can find out no rhyme to 'lady' but 'baby' – an innocent rhyme; for 'scorn', 'horn' – a hard rhyme; for 'school', 'fool' – a babbling rhyme; very ominous endings. No, I was not born under a rhyming planet, nor I cannot woo in festival terms.   39

Enter BEATRICE

Sweet Beatrice, wouldst thou come when I called thee?

BEATRICE: Yea signor, and depart when you bid me.

BENEDICK: O stay but till then.

BEATRICE: 'Then' is spoken. Fare you well now – and yet ere I go, let me go with that I came for, which is with knowing what hath passed between you and Claudio.

BENEDICK: Only foul words – and thereupon I will kiss thee.

BEATRICE: Foul words is but foul wind, and foul wind is but foul breath, and foul breath is noisome, therefore I will depart unkissed.   50

BENEDICK: Thou hast frighted the word out of his right sense, so forcible is thy wit. But I must tell thee plainly, Claudio undergoes my challenge, and either I must shortly hear from him, or I will subscribe him a coward. And I pray thee now tell me for which of my bad parts didst thou first fall in love with me?

BEATRICE: For them all together, which maintained so politic a state of evil that they will not admit any good part to intermingle with them. But for which of my good parts did you first suffer love for me?   60

63   *In spite of*, (a) against, (b) in despising.

67–70 *there's ... neighbours.* Proverbially 'he who praises himself has ill
neighbours'. Either his neighbours shun him or he is unworthy
of their esteem. Benedick asserts that men must sing their own
praise since good neighbours no longer exist to do it for them.

71–2 *he ... monument*, i.e. his memory will last no longer.

74   *Question*, a question indeed.

75   *rheum*, tears.

76   *Don ... conscience.* Conscience was commonly regarded as gnaw-
ing inside a man. See *Isaiah*, lxvi.24, *Mark*, ix.44–8. *Don*, master.
worm, snake, maggot.

84–5 *There ... too.* Do they spring apart from an embrace?

87   *old coil*, tremendous to do. *old*, very much.

90   *presently*, at once.

92–3 *I ... eyes*, i.e. I give myself to you utterly.

BENEDICK: Suffer love! A good epithet. I do suffer love indeed, for I love thee against my will.

BEATRICE: In spite of your heart, I think; alas poor heart! If you spite it for my sake, I will spite it for yours, for I will never love that which my friend hates.

BENEDICK: Thou and I are too wise to woo peaceably.

BEATRICE: It appears not in this confession; there's not one wise man among twenty that will praise himself.   68

BENEDICK: An old, an old instance Beatrice, that lived in the time of good neighbours. If a man do not erect in this age his own tomb ere he dies, he shall live no longer in monument than the bell rings and the widow weeps.

BEATRICE: And how long is that, think you?

BENEDICK: Question. Why, an hour in clamour and a quarter in rheum. Therefore is it most expedient for the wise, if Don Worm, his conscience, find no impediment to the contrary, to be the trumpet of his own virtues, as I am to myself. So much for praising myself, who I myself will bear witness is praiseworthy. And now tell me, how doth your cousin?   80

BEATRICE: Very ill.

BENEDICK: And how do you?

BEATRICE: Very ill too.

BENEDICK: Serve God, love me, and mend. There will I leave you too, for here comes one in haste.

Enter URSULA

URSULA: Madam, you must come to your uncle. Yonder's old coil at home. It is proved my Lady Hero hath been falsely accused, the Prince and Claudio mightily abused, and Don John is the author of all, who is fled and gone. Will you come presently?   90

BEATRICE: Will you go hear this news signor?

BENEDICK: I will live in thy heart, die in thy lap, and be

Margaret is re-established. Benedick and Beatrice gently tease each other, their 'merry war' is in a kindlier key. Finally it is clear that the duel will not take place.

A churchyard

In order to give this scene substance and emotional impact and to avoid triviality there should be full ritual, ceremonial movement, and genuflexion.

Properties required – torches or tapers, garlands, paper scrolls (epitaphs).

.D.   F adds 'all wearing mourning'. Where are the musicians placed?

5   *guerdon*, recompense.
6   *fame*, reputation, honour.

10   *dumb* F. Q has 'dead'.

;.D.   *Song*. The singer is not named, but Balthasar, who sings at II.iii.58, is the likely singer. He has therefore been brought in at the beginning of the scene with the musicians.

12   *goddess . . . night*. Diana was goddess of the moon and of virginity. She was also depicted as the goddess of hunting with virgins as her armed attendants.

16   *moan*, lament.
17   *groan*, grief.

buried in thy eyes. And moreover, I will go with thee to
thy uncle's.   [*Exeunt*

SCENE THREE

Enter CLAUDIO, DON PEDRO *and three or four
with tapers,* BALTHASAR *and musicians*

CLAUDIO: Is this the monument of Leonato?
A LORD: It is, my lord.
CLAUDIO: [*Reading from a scroll*]

Epitaph
Done to death by slanderous tongues
    Was the Hero that here lies;
Death, in guerdon of her wrongs,
    Gives her fame which never dies.
So the life that died with shame
Lives in death with glorious fame.
    Hang thou there upon the tomb,
    Praising her when I am dumb.   10
Now music sound, and sing your solemn hymn.

Song

BALTHASAR:
            Pardon, goddess of the night,
            Those that slew thy virgin knight,
            For the which with songs of woe,
            Round about her tomb they go.
            Midnight assist our moan,
            Help us to sigh and groan,
                Heavily, heavily.

195

20   *uttered*, expressed, commemorated in song.

25   *The ... preyed.* Perhaps a suggestion that not only have the wolves ceased their preying, but that the tragic and evil things are now over.

26   *wheels of Phoebus*, the wheels of the sun-god's chariot.

29   *several*, separate.

30   *weeds*, clothes.

32   *Hymen*, god of marriage. *speeds*, prospers.

Some see dramatic irony in this scene. The dirge sung at Hero's tomb takes the place of the serenade that was prepared for Hero's wedding eve (II.iii.82–4). It serves to expiate the discordant aspects of the play, and to prepare for the harmonious conclusion.

Leonato's house

S.D.   Leonato, Friar, Benedick and Antonio enter together, the ladies perhaps from a different door.

2–3   *So ... debated.* Do you agree?

3   *debated*, discussed.

7   *sort*, turn out.

8   *by faith*, by honour.

Graves yawn and yield your dead,
Till death be uttered, 20
Heavily, heavily.

CLAUDIO: Now, unto thy bones good night.
Yearly will I do this rite.

DON PEDRO: Good morrow masters, put your torches out.
The wolves have preyed, and look, the gentle day,
Before the wheels of Phoebus, round about
Dapples the drowsy east with spots of grey.
Thanks to you all, and leave us. Fare you well.

CLAUDIO: Good morrow masters. Each his several way.

DON PEDRO: Come let us hence, and put on other weeds,
And then to Leonato's we will go. 31

CLAUDIO: And Hymen now with luckier issue speeds
Than this for whom we rendered up this woe.

[*Exeunt*

SCENE FOUR

Enter LEONATO, ANTONIO, BENEDICK, BEATRICE,
MARGARET, URSULA, FRIAR FRANCIS, *and* HERO

FRIAR: Did I not tell you she was innocent?

LEONATO: So are the Prince and Claudio, who accused her
Upon the error that you heard debated.
But Margaret was in some fault for this,
Although against her will, as it appears
In the true course of all the question.

ANTONIO: Well, I am glad that all things sort so well.

BENEDICK: And so am I, being else by faith enforced
To call young Claudio to a reckoning for it.

LEONATO: Well daughter, and you gentlewomen all, 10

14   *office*, part.

17   *confirmed countenance*, (a) straight face, (b) convincing authority.
18   *entreat your pains*, trouble you to do something.

20   *bind*, (a) marry, (b) tie up. *undo*, (a) release, (b) ruin.

23   *eye ... her*, i.e. she saw when Hero's description in the arbour scene
        opened her eyes.
25–6   *The ... Prince*. See II.iii.
27   *enigmatical*, obscure, puzzling.

36   *yet*, still.

38   *Ethiope*, black, ugly.

Withdraw into a chamber by yourselves,
And when I send for you come hither masked.
The Prince and Claudio promised by this hour
To visit me. You know your office brother –
You must be father to your brother's daughter,
And give her to young Claudio.   [*Exeunt Ladies*

ANTONIO: Which I will do with confirmed countenance.

BENEDICK: Friar, I must entreat your pains, I think.

FRIAR: To do what signor?

BENEDICK: To bind me, or undo me – one of them.   20
    Signor Leonato, truth it is good signor,
    Your niece regards me with an eye of favour.

LEONATO: That eye my daughter lent her, 'tis most true.

BENEDICK: And I do with an eye of love requite her.

LEONATO: The sight whereof I think you had from me,
    From Claudio, and the Prince. But what's your will?

BENEDICK: Your answer sir is enigmatical;
    But for my will, my will is, your good will
    May stand with ours, this day to be conjoined
    In the state of honourable marriage –   30
    In which, good Friar, I shall desire your help.

LEONATO: My heart is with your liking.

FRIAR: And my help.
    Here comes the Prince and Claudio.

Enter DON PEDRO *and* CLAUDIO, *and two or three others*

DON PEDRO: Good morrow to this fair assembly.

LEONATO: Good morrow Prince. Good morrow Claudio.
    We here attend you. Are you yet determined
    Today to marry with my brother's daughter?

CLAUDIO: I'll hold my mind were she an Ethiope.

LEONATO: Call her forth brother. Here's the Friar ready.
                                        [*Exit Antonio*

40-2 *Why ... cloudiness?* Why is Benedick disapproving?

43 *savage bull.* See I.i.232-8; V.i.172-5.
44 *tip ... gold*, i.e. make a festival offering of you as a prime cuckold.

46 *Europa.* In classical story the daughter of the king of Phoenecia who, while playing on the sea-shore, was carried off to Crete by Jupiter in the shape of a bull.

52 *I owe you*, I'll pay you back. *reck'nings*, i.e. in which he is being paid book, or, things to deal with.

67 *qualify*, moderate, put in perspective.

DON PEDRO: Good morrow Benedick. Why what's the
    matter, 40
  That you have such a February face,
  So full of frost, of storm, and cloudiness?
CLAUDIO: I think he thinks upon the savage bull.
  Tush fear not man, we'll tip thy horns with gold,
  And all Europa shall rejoice at thee,
  As once Europa did at lusty Jove,
  When he would play the noble beast in love.
BENEDICK: Bull Jove sir, had an amiable low,
  And some such strange bull leaped your father's cow,
  And got a calf in that same noble feat 50
  Much like to you, for you have just his bleat.
CLAUDIO: For this I owe you. Here comes other reck'nings.

Enter ANTONIO, *with the Ladies masked*

  Which is the lady I must seize upon?
ANTONIO: This same is she, and I do give you her.
CLAUDIO: Why then she's mine. Sweet, let me see your
    face.
ANTONIO: No, that you shall not till you take her hand
  Before this Friar, and swear to marry her.
CLAUDIO: Give me your hand before this holy Friar;
  I am your husband, if you like of me. 59
HERO: [*Unmasks*] And when I lived I was your other wife;
  And when you loved, you were my other husband.
CLAUDIO: Another Hero!
HERO: Nothing certainer.
  One Hero died defiled, but I do live,
  And surely as I live, I am a maid.
DON PEDRO: The former Hero! Hero that is dead!
LEONATO: She died my lord, but whiles her slander lived.
FRIAR: All this amazement can I qualify,
  When after that the holy rites are ended,

69 *largely*, in full.
70 *let ... familiar*, treat everything as normal.

83 *but ... recompense*, only as friend to friend.

87 *halting*, i.e. with imperfect feet.

96 *in a consumption*, pining away.

I'll tell you largely of fair Hero's death.
Meantime let wonder seem familiar,   70
And to the chapel let us presently.

BENEDICK: Soft and fair, Friar. Which is Beatrice?

BEATRICE: [*Unmasks*] I answer to that name. What is your will?

BENEDICK: Do not you love me?

BEATRICE: Why no, no more than reason.

BENEDICK: Why then your uncle, and the Prince, and Claudio
Have been deceived, they swore you did.

BEATRICE: Do not you love me?

BENEDICK: Troth no, no more than reason.

BEATRICE: Why then my cousin, Margaret, and Ursula
Are much deceived, for they did swear you did.   79

BENEDICK: They swore that you were almost sick for me.

BEATRICE: They swore that you were well-nigh dead for me.

BENEDICK: 'Tis no such matter. Then you do not love me?

BEATRICE: No truly, but in friendly recompense.

LEONATO: Come cousin, I am sure you love the gentleman.

CLAUDIO: And I'll be sworn upon't that he loves her,
For here's a paper written in his hand,
A halting sonnet of his own pure brain,
Fashioned to Beatrice.

HERO: And here's another
Writ in my cousin's hand, stolen from her pocket,
Containing her affection unto Benedick.   90

BENEDICK: A miracle! Here's our own hands against our hearts. Come, I will have thee, but by this light I take thee for pity.

BEATRICE: I would not deny you, but by this good day, I yield upon great persuasion, and partly to save your life, for I was told you were in a consumption.

100   *flout*, mock.

101–3 *if ... him*, if a man allows himself to be upset by jokes at his expense, he will certainly not dare to wear fine clothes, much less marry a beautiful woman.

102   *beaten with brains*, attacked with witticisms.

112   *double-dealer*, (a) cheat, i.e. unfaithful, (b) married man as opposed to single man.

113–14 *look ... thee*, keep a close watch on you.

119   *First ... word.* Benedick overrules Leonato – why?

120   *sad*, serious, melancholy.

121   *staff*, (a) emblem of authority, (b) symbol of old age. *tipped with horn*, i.e. cuckold.

125   *brave*, fine, apt. *pipers*. No entry is given for them. Are they placed in a music room above stage, or should they come on stage?

s.d.   *Dance.* What kind of dance would be appropriate – pavane, jig, lavolta, galliard?

BENEDICK: [*Kisses her*] Peace, I will stop your mouth.

DON PEDRO: How dost thou, Benedick the married man?

BENEDICK: I'll tell thee what Prince. A college of wit-crackers cannot flout me out of my humour. Dost thou think I care for a satire or an epigram? No, if a man will be beaten with brains, 'a shall wear nothing handsome about him. In brief, since I do purpose to marry, I will think nothing to any purpose that the world can say against it; and therefore never flout at me for what I have said against it. For man is a giddy thing, and this is my conclusion. For thy part Claudio, I did think to have beaten thee, but in that thou art like to be my kinsman, live unbruised, and love my cousin.   109

CLAUDIO: I had well hoped thou wouldst have denied Beatrice, that I might have cudgelled thee out of thy single life, to make thee a double-dealer, which out of question thou wilt be, if my cousin do not look exceeding narrowly to thee.

BENEDICK: Come, come, we are friends. Let's have a dance ere we are married, that we may lighten our own hearts and our wives' heels.

LEONATO: We'll have dancing afterward.

BENEDICK: First, of my word, therefore play music. Prince, thou art sad; get thee a wife, get thee a wife; there is no staff more reverend than one tipped with horn.   121

Enter a Messenger

MESSENGER: My lord, your brother John is ta'en in flight, And brought with armed men back to Messina.

BENEDICK: Think not on him till tomorrow; I'll devise thee brave punishments for him. Strike up pipers.

[*Dance, and then exeunt*

APPENDICES

I

SOURCES

THE romantic Claudio–Hero plot is based on dramatic and narrative versions of a story in Ariosto's romantic epic *Orlando Furioso* (1516). The extant dramatic versions – there were two other English plays not now extant – did not influence Shakespeare much. He may have owed the name Beatrice to the witty maid in Pasqualigo's version *Il Fedele* (1597), and the idea of comic constables who utter malapropisms to the same play, or to Anthony Munday's English version, *Fedele and Fortunio* (1585).

Orlando Furioso in Italian, Harington's English version (1591) and a variant in Bandello's *Novelle* (1554) provided Shakespeare with the material. In these versions the hero is deceived by a rival into believing that the heroine is unfaithful. In Ariosto's version a maid, in love with the villainous rival, dresses in her mistress's clothes to receive her lover at the window without realizing that she is being used to betray her mistress. Bandello's version, here summarized, is closer to *Much Ado About Nothing*.

Timbreo, a wealthy young courtier at the court of King Piero of Aragon, then in Messina, falls in love with Fenecia, daughter of Lionato, the head of a socially inferior but honourable family. Unwilling to marry an inferior, he seeks to seduce her, but she virtuously resists his approaches. Thereupon through an intermediary he offers her marriage. His close friend Girondo also falls in love with Fenecia, and, hoping to prevent the marriage and win Fenecia for himself, he employs a courtier to demonstrate to Timbreo that Fenecia is unchaste. The courtier places a ladder outside an unused room in Fenecia's house. Timbreo sees a courtier mount the ladder and hears him speak apparently to Fenecia. Timbreo immediately assumes that Fenecia is unchaste though in fact she was not in the room. He sends his intermediary to Fenecia's father to break off the marriage. Fenecia swoons and is given out as dead. Her father sends her into the country hoping to marry her under another name when things have quietened down.

Believing Fenecia to be dead, Timbreo and Girondo are filled with remorse. Girondo confesses his treachery and, before Fenecia's tomb, offers his dagger to Timbreo inviting him to exact revenge. Timbreo forgives him, and the two confess their wrongdoing to Lionato. They are forgiven on condition that Timbreo marries a bride of Lionato's choosing. Timbreo does not at first recognize his bride as Fenecia, so much has she changed. Girondo marries Fenecia's sister Belfiore.

Shakespeare redirects the story. The main theme of the source story is love versus friendship. This theme briefly appears as a result of Don John's first plot (II.i.157–8), and is then discarded completely. So, in place of friends who become rivals, Shakespeare has Claudio, a young courtier, favoured by Don Pedro. The latter honourably and successfully woos Hero on behalf of Claudio; any notions of Hero's inferiority and of treacherous rivalry are transferred to Don John's plot to create discord. Claudio does not try to seduce Hero, on the contrary he is inspired by her modesty, and he treats her with 'Bashful sincerity and comely love'. Shakespeare creates Don John as the sole source of evil. In this way neither Don Pedro nor Claudio is tainted with originating evil.

Shakespeare seems intent on the theme of the 'honourable estate' of matrimony.

II

Note on II.i.179–80

Ho! Now you strike like the blind man; 'twas the boy that stole your meat, and you'll beat the post.

Editors take this as an allusion to an incident in a Spanish novel, *Lazarillo de Tormes*, which narrates the adventures of a boy of that name. The novel was printed in English in 1586.

The boy steals sausages from his master, a blind man, who detects the smell of sausages on the boy and punishes him severely. The boy in revenge leads the blind man to a river, invites him to jump over, after placing him in front of a post. The blind man jumps, hits the post, and falls half dead. The boy mocks him, 'You could smell the sausages but not the post'.

There are clear resemblances to Shakespeare's version but equally clear differences which prompt the view that the allusion derives from French farces. As early as the thirteenth century the blind man and his boy were subjects of French farces, in varying versions of which the boy stole money, sausage, cloak, and wench from the blind man. French farces were known and adapted in England early in the sixteenth century, and it is possible that incidents from them or extemporized versions remained in popular memory. Edward Burrough who has examined French farces suggests privately: 'I could imagine a version where the blind man discovers his loss of money and cloak (and sausage), he lays about him with a stick, and the wicked boy could have hung the stolen cloak on a post to deceive him into thinking he is on target.' It seems a reasonable guess.

III

SHAKESPEARE'S THEATRE

ALTHOUGH the evidence for the design of Elizabethan theatres is incomplete and conflicting, and although there were certainly differences of construction and arrangement, the following account, it is hoped, will give a reasonable outline.

The first public theatres in London were built during Shakespeare's lifetime. According to some they embodied in their design and construction the experience and practice of the medieval and Tudor play productions in inn yards, booth stages, and pageant wagons. Recently Glynne Wickham has argued strongly against this view, claiming that the game-houses, tournament arenas, banqueting chamber, and town hall provide the basis for Elizabethan stages both in public theatres and in banqueting rooms (*Early English Stages*, II, Pt I, p. 267).

From square, circular, or hexagonal theatre walls tiered with galleries for spectators, the Elizabethan stage jutted out over six feet above ground level and occupied about half the floor space where the spectators could stand on three sides of it. The stage of the Fortune theatre was 43 feet × 27 feet and the floor area in which it stood was 55 feet × 55 feet. At the back of the stage the lowest tier of spectators' galleries gave place to a curtained recess or inner stage, a space used for concealment, discovery of characters sleeping or studying, or for holding stage properties in readiness. Another view is that there was no recess, but a curtained space under a canopy in front of the rear wall of the stage. On either side were dressing rooms from which entrance doors opened on to the stage. The first floor gallery behind the stage was used for scenes in the play; a second floor gallery or room was used by musicians. Above the balcony and covering the rear portion of the stage was a canopy or roof painted blue and adorned with stars sometimes supported by pillars from the stage. There were trapdoors in the stage and frequently a low rail around it. The pillars, canopy, railings, and back stage were painted and adorned. If a tragedy was to be performed, the stage was hung with black, but there was no set staging in the modern fashion.

It has been argued very strongly by I. A. Shapiro (*Shakespeare Studies*, 2, Cincinnati, 1966, pp. 192–209) that the woodcut of the memory theatre in Fludd's *Ars Memoriæ*, which F. Yates suggested in her *Art of Memory* was a representation of the second Globe theatre, is rather a representation of the private Blackfriars theatre where *Antony and Cleopatra* was at one time produced. Yates expanded her views in *Theatre of the World*, 1969. It will be noticed that there is a chamber projecting from the middle of the balcony backstage, the balcony having entrances at both ends. Such a construction would greatly facilitate the raising of Antony into the monument (*Antony and Cleopatra*, IV.xv).

There were stage properties usually of the kind that could be easily pushed on and off the stage. Records of the time mention a mossy bank, a wall, a bed, trees, arbours, thrones, tents, rock, tomb, hell-mouth, a cauldron; on the other hand tents, pavilions, and mansions may have been permanent 'sets' in some historical plays. These structures varied in size for a small one may have sufficed for the tomb in *Romeo and Juliet*, but the tent representing the Queen's chamber in Peele's *Edward I* contained six adults and a bed. On the whole properties were limited to essentials although the popularity of the private masques with their painted canvas sets encouraged increasing elaboration of scenery and spectacle during the reign of James I.

There was no limitation to the display of rich and gorgeous costumes in the current fashion of the day. The more magnificent and splendid the better; indeed the costumes must have been the most expensive item in the requirements of the company. An occasional attempt was made at period costume, but normally plays were produced in Elizabethan garments without any suspicion of the oddness that strikes us when we read of Cæsar entering 'in his nightgown', or Cleopatra calling on Charmian to cut the lace of what we may call her corsets. High rank was marked by magnificence of dress, a trade or calling by functional clothes. Feste, the clown, would wear the traditional fool's coat or petticoat of motley, a coarse cloth of mixed yellow and green. The coat

A WOODCUT FROM R. FLUDD'S
Ars Memoriæ
possibly representing the Blackfriars Theatre

was buttoned from the neck to the girdle from which hung a wooden dagger, its skirts voluminous with capacious pockets in which Feste might 'impetticoat' any 'gratillity'. Ghosts, who appear in a number of plays, usually wore a kind of leathern smock. Oberon and magicians such as Prospero wore, in the delightful phrase and spelling of the records, 'a robe for to goo invisibell'.

The actors formed companies under the patronage of noblemen for protection against civic law condemning them as 'rogues, vagabonds and sturdy beggars' to severe punishment. They were the servants of their patron and wore his livery. The company was a co-operative society, its members jointly owned the property and shared the profits; thus Shakespeare's plays were not his to use as he liked, they belonged to his company, the Lord Chamberlain's Men. This company, honoured by James I when it became the King's Men, was the most successful company of the period. It had a number of distinguished actors, it achieved more Court performances than any other company, and it performed in the best London theatre, the Globe, until it was burnt down during a performance of *Henry VIII* in 1613. Women were not allowed on the public stage, although they performed in masques and theatricals in private houses. Boys, therefore, were apprenticed to the leading actors and took the female parts.

An almost unbelievable number of plays was produced by the companies. It has been shown for example that in a fortnight eleven performances of ten different plays were presented by one company at one theatre. The companies were in effect repertory companies. Their productions consisted of new plays, and old plays either repeated without change, or revised sometimes extensively. It is to be wondered how far the actors achieved word-perfection in their parts. Their versatility and their team work no doubt helped to overcome the burden of such rapid changes of parts. Indeed although the main parts in a play were performed by a small select group of actors, there is little evidence of typecasting apart from the clowns, or that plays were written with particular actors in mind.

The audience in the public theatres was drawn from all classes.

There were courtiers and inns of court men who appreciated intricate word play, mythological allusions, and the technique of sword play; there were the 'groundlings' who liked jigs, horseplay, and flamboyance of speech and spectacle; and there were the citizens who appreciated the romantic stories, the high eloquence of patriotic plays, and moral sentiments. A successful play would have something for all. In private theatres like the Blackfriars gallants would sit on a stool on the stage and behave rather like the

Courtesy of the British Council

MODEL OF AN ELIZABETHAN THEATRE
by Richard Southern

courtiers in *A Midsummer Night's Dream*, V.i, or *Love's Labour's Lost*, V.ii. The 'groundlings' too were likely to be troublesome and noisy. They could buy bottled beer, oranges, and nuts for their comfort; but it is noted to their credit that when Falstaff appeared on the stage, so popular was he that they stopped cracking nuts! They applauded a well delivered speech; they hissed a boring play; they even rioted and severely damaged one theatre. Shakespeare's plays however were popular among all classes: at Court they

> did so take Eliza and our James,

and elsewhere in the public theatre they outshone the plays of other dramatists. Any play of his was assured of a 'full house'. An ardent theatre-goer of the day praising Shakespeare's plays above those of other dramatists wrote:

> When let but Falstaff come,
> Hal, Poins, the rest, you scarce shall have a room,
> All is so pester'd; let but Beatrice
> And Benedick be seen, lo in a trice
> The cockpit, galleries, boxes, all are full
> To hear Malvolio, that cross-garter'd gull.

The best in classic and

Jane Austen

Elizabeth Laird

Beverley Naidoo Roddy Doyle

Robert Swindells

George Orwell

Charles Dickens

Charlotte Brontë

Jan Mark

Anne Fine

Anthony Horowitz